"Surprise Sithole is a modern-day apostle who is literally changing Africa. You will be thrilled and blessed with his life stories that will literally change you!"

John Arnott, president, Catch the Fire, Toronto

"Surprise Sithole is an international co-leader with Iris Global, as well as a great friend. Over the years he has been a tremendous blessing and encouragement to us personally as well as the Iris family in Africa and around the world. His book, *Voice in the Night*, is full of miracle stories that will encourage and fill you with fresh faith. As you read this book, prepare to be greatly inspired and begin to step into your own miracle-working inheritance in Jesus!"

Rolland and Heidi Baker, founding directors, Iris Global

"I thank God that I have had the privilege of meeting Surprise Sithole. He walks in the greatest joy of any person I have ever met, and his story is the most amazing story I have ever heard. Through *Voice in the Night*, you now have the same privilege of listening to Surprise's story."

Randy Clark, president and founder, Global Awakening; overseer, Apostolic Network of Global Awakening; founder, Global School of Supernatural Ministry

Voice
in the
Night

Voice in the Night

The True Story of A MAN and THE MIRACLES That
Are CHANGING AFRICA

Pastor Surprise
with David Wimbish

Chosen

a division of Baker Publishing Group
Minneapolis, Minnesota

Published by Chosen Books
11400 Hampshire Avenue South
Bloomington, Minnesota 55438
www.chosenbooks.com

Chosen Books is a division of
Baker Publishing Group, Grand Rapids, Michigan

Printed in the United States of America

Library of Congress Cataloging-in-Publication Data
Surprise, Pastor.
    Voice in the night : the true story of a man and the miracles that are changing Africa / Pastor Surprise with David Wimbish.
        p. cm.
    ISBN 978-0-8007-9523-8 (pbk. : alk. paper)
    1. Surprise, Pastor. 2. Christian biography—Africa. 3. Christianity—Africa.
I. Wimbish, David. II. Title.
BR1720.S87A3 2012
269′.2092—dc23   2011040695
[B]

Cover design by Dan Pitts

12   13   14   15   16   17   18   7   6   5   4   3   2   1

To my wonderful wife: You are my best friend, and my journey would have been truly lonely without you. Thank you for encouraging and supporting me to travel and spread the Gospel. You are one of God's great gifts to me, and I love you very much.

To my boys, Enoch, Love, Israel and Blessing: I am proud of you, and I want to thank you for your love and for supporting me as much as you have. When I am away, I long to return to be with you, to have fun with you and to watch you grow strong in the Lord.

To Susan Partridge and her family: You have been like gold to me and to my family. Your words of encouragement and your prophetic words over my life have all been deeply accurate. Thank you—thank you for walking with me on this journey in life, and thank you for your kindness. May the Lord give you long life. May He give you joy, and may you walk into your destiny. May the Lord lift you up. Amen.

Contents

Contents

Foreword

Surprise Sithole is one of the most amazing individuals I have ever met. His closest friends say he is *depression challenged*, which is a humorous way of saying he is the happiest person we know. His story is a God story from beginning to end. It is filled with supernatural interventions in which God demonstrates who this wonderful man belongs to. And while he is quick to say his story is about the grace of his wonderful Savior, Jesus Christ, it rightfully includes the story of the man who said the absolute *yes* to God. And for this I am eternally grateful—grateful to be able to watch a life poured out for the glory of God. Grateful to see God defend and protect one of His own so openly.

I love to hear the testimonies of God's call upon a person's life. Both the Bible and our history books are filled with stories of people's defining moments with God. They range from very subtle encounters all the way to the extreme; yet in His sovereignty God alone chooses how to manifest Himself to each person. I have noticed that the more extreme a person's initial call from God, the more challenging circumstances they will face in carrying out that call. One could not argue with this fact in the apostle Paul's life following his Damascus Road experience. The same is true with Surprise Sithole. The son of two witch doctors, he awoke one night to God's voice commanding him to leave his house. And so the adventure began so many years ago, and the journey continues to this day. Seldom will you read of one so uniquely chosen by God as you will in *Voice in the Night*.

If there is such a thing as godly jealousy, and I believe there is, you are about to face it head-on. I cannot imagine reading this story without becoming extremely hungry for all that God has for us at any price. Some books are so captivating that you are sad when they end; that is how I felt on the last page of this book. This is one time I wished I had been reading a five-hundred-page book.

Read *Voice in the Night* to learn. Or read it to be inspired. Even read it to grow in faith. Just read it. This book is bound to leave a mark on your life.

Bill Johnson
Bethel Church, Redding, California
Author, *When Heaven Invades Earth*
and *Face to Face with God*

Acknowledgments

I want to thank all those who have supported me on this journey of mine, some of whom I have mentioned and many I have not—all my staff, all the wonderful pastors who have trusted and worked with me around the world and all those who have helped me on my way.

My thanks to Susan Partridge for all her involvement and input and for making this book happen. I honor her so much for that. Thanks to Liz Batha for her hard work in researching this book and to Geraldine Streather, who has helped in the proofreading process.

I also want to thank my friends Rolland and Heidi Baker. First to Rolland because you have been special to me indeed as we traveled together through the bush discussing the things of life. You have influenced my life hugely, and I have learned from and been inspired greatly by you. I want to thank God that as we stood together through your sickness, He healed you and now you are well. I thank God for that, and I am looking forward to working with you again as we help spread the Gospel through your life.

And to Heidi: Thank you, because I have learned about love through you. I have learned about love beyond discrimination, and I have learned courage and a life of giving. And I just want to thank you.

1

A Voice in the Night

Surprise!"

The voice boomed in my ear, rousing me from a deep sleep. I blinked, trying to see who could be calling my name at this hour of the night, but it was pitch dark inside my family's hut. I could not see a thing.

I lay there for a moment, listening to the sound of my heart pounding in my chest. Had I been dreaming? It had seemed so real.

"Surprise!"

The voice was louder and more insistent than before. I sat up. "Yes? Who are you? What do you want?"

The voice was masculine, strong and deep. "Get out of the house. If you do not leave, you will die."

I opened my mouth to reply, but nothing came out.

"Surprise! You must leave. Now!"

The command was so loud and urgent that the earth beneath me seemed to tremble. I felt that everyone in my village would probably come running to see what was going on at our home—but nobody else seemed to be able to hear the voice. My father's snoring told me he was still asleep. My mother and my sister Maria did not stir.

I was fifteen years old and not at all ready to face the world on my own. But I knew I could not ignore this powerful, commanding voice. I jumped up, dressed quickly and walked out into the African night. I didn't know where I was going or what was about to happen to my family. I only knew that my life was at stake.

I have not been back to my village or seen my parents since that night, over 25 years ago.

Before I share the rest of the story, I want you to know more about me. I grew up a very poor child in an impoverished village called Cachote in rural Mozambique. I had never heard of Jesus Christ.

Although I now believe it was God Himself who spoke to me on that night long ago, I can think of no earthly reason why He should have intervened in my life in such a dramatic way. I just know He did.

My parents were witch doctors, as were my grandparents before them. My mother and father claimed to be in touch with ancient spirits who were wise and powerful. I sometimes saw their power, but I never would have described them as wise. Instead, they seemed mean and capricious. They delighted in revenge and stirred up trouble between neighbors and didn't seem to mind that my parents used them to make money from other people's misfortunes.

Sadly, this was the only spiritual reality I knew, although I longed for something more. It seemed clear that the puny spirits my parents invoked through their magical incantations had not created the world around me. They did not make the mighty lion, the ferocious crocodile, the dense jungle that surrounded our village, the bright stars that filled the sky above me at night.

Sometimes, when I looked up at those stars, I felt a sense of awe and peace of mind that momentarily lifted me above the difficulties of life in my impoverished village. But I did not look up often enough.

Despite my parents' status as witch doctors, my family was terribly poor. But then, so was everyone else in my village. All the children I knew lived in small one- or two-room huts constructed of thatch and mud. At night we all slept on thin reed mats unrolled over the dirt floor. Our mothers prepared food—when there was food to prepare—over stone hearth fires that filled our homes with smoke. Those fires also kept us warm at night and in the wintertime as we huddled so close to the fire pit that our legs were burned by embers that were spit in our direction.

Like the other families in our village, we spent most of our time outside. We went inside to sleep or in an attempt to stay dry when it rained, but we did not live inside the way westerners do.

Sometimes, when there had not been sufficient rain to grow food—or when there had been too much rain—we survived by eating the leaves of cassava or pumpkin. They tasted terrible, as you would expect. But I was often hungry enough that I was glad to get them.

Another "meal" I detested was something my mother called "chicken stew," although there was no chicken in it. Really, it was just salty hot water. Chicken or any other type of meat was a rare luxury for my family. If we were lucky enough to have it, we would receive a tiny piece about the size of a fingertip. But we were not to eat it. Instead, we were to place it under our noses to get the scent of it before each sip of saltwater. The idea, of course, was to flavor the "stew," but it didn't work. In this way we sipped our stew until, at the very end, we could finally eat the morsel of chicken or goat.

October and November were the worst months for hunger, when the food from the previous harvest was gone and it was difficult to find anything to eat in the jungle. In desperation, some would make the three-hour walk to the crocodile-infested Shire River to collect water lily bulbs. This was a dangerous business, and many were killed by the crocs. They had chosen a quick, violent death over a slow, painful death from starvation.

My village was composed of a small circle of huts situated in a clearing in the Mozambican jungle. I was the last of seven children, living in a world far away from things like telephones or television. We had no running water or electricity. The nearest medical clinic was nearly a day's walk away. Two of my sisters died before my parents could get help for them. They had appealed to the spirits for healing, but none came. There were no roads into or out of our village—just rutted dirt trails. By the time the voice called me to leave my family, Maria and I were the only two children still living at home, as we were the youngest.

How I Got My Name

People often ask me how I came to be named Surprise. It is because I was born with a small patch of white hair. My parents were surprised when they saw it, and that is how I got my name. Westerners often smile or laugh when they hear my name for the first time. But Surprise does not get that sort of reaction in Africa; there, names almost always have specific meanings.

In fact, my parents had intended to name me Try, because they were trying to have another boy. But they changed their minds when they saw that white hair. Perhaps they thought it was an omen, marking me as a special child with powers I could use to carry on the family business. But God had other plans for me.

My father was tall and thin with hair that sprouted in all directions. He had a kind heart, often bringing home children who had been orphaned and other children he had rescued from various plights common to the jungle. He took in a boy named Jalenti, who was orphaned at the age of two when his father died of leprosy. Poor Jalenti also had leprosy, and we had to build him a shelter in the woods to protect ourselves from the disease. Purple splotches covered his skin, and his hair fell out in clumps, leaving big bald areas on his head. It fell to me to take his food into the jungle and then pull on a little cord so he would know he could come get it. Jalenti's sad life came to a tragic end when he was given medication to treat his leprosy and died after drinking it all at once.

The fact that my father took Jalenti in shows his kindness. And yet, like most fathers in my culture, to his own children he was a distant authority figure.

My favorite memories of him all revolve around fishing, during the years when there had been sufficient rainfall to fill the nearby river. He would bring his long *konga* basket, and we would walk through the jungle together. I remember trying hard to keep up with him as he strode toward the river wearing his traditional *kaplana*, a brightly colored cloth wrapped around his midsection. We did not have much to say to each other, but I was happy just to be with him. Of course, there was another reason for my happiness: If we caught some fish, we would not be eating cassava leaves or "chicken stew" for dinner.

I also spent some time alone with my mother, deep in the jungle, looking for herbs she and my father could use in their magical elixirs and potions. Some of the herbs my mother and I collected on our trips would be used immediately, while others would be dried and kept in round reed baskets under my parents' *dalimba*, the makeshift bed that represented the only piece of furniture in our hut.

My mother was of a rather stout build, with lighter skin than my father. She wore her hair tied back with a piece of cloth, and she was extensively "tattooed," meaning that her skin had been cut on her stomach, arms and thighs to make her more beautiful. All of the older girls and women in our village had similar tattoos. One time I came out of the jungle and saw my mother giving a teenaged girl a beauty treatment by cutting the skin of her stomach. The girl, obviously in pain, clinched a stick between her teeth to keep from crying out. Even in the jungle there was competition for attention, and girls were willing to suffer to make themselves more attractive.

My mother was not happy about my father's penchant for bringing home company unannounced. She had enough trouble trying to fill the hungry stomachs of her own children. Neither did she like my father's drinking. He would often come home late at night, drunk on a local brew and calling out the name of his deceased sister. "Fina! Fina!" he would cry. This only made my mother more annoyed. She felt that my father was always comparing her unfavorably to his late sister, whom he described as "the most caring person I ever knew."

Life was hard for my mother. She sometimes went without food so her children could eat—and she had no hope that things would ever get better.

She and my father fought constantly. I will never forget the time, when I was a very small child, that my mother hurled the corn-pounding stick at my father, cutting his forehead so badly that blood streamed down his face. I ran away crying and tried to hide under the bed. I felt that it was all my father's fault, and I wanted to tell my mother that we could run away and start a new life somewhere. But where? And how? It was impossible, so I held my tongue. Like my mother, I was becoming resigned to a life without hope.

Keeping the "Thieves" Away

Most of my time was spent watching over our small crops of cassava and maize and our other crops—doing my best to keep the birds, monkeys and other pests away. Every afternoon after school, and during weekends and holidays, I went out to the fields, waited underneath the shelter my father had built and waved my hands and shouted at any thieves who happened to show up. We had tried to keep the birds away with a scarecrow, but they did not fall for it. In fact, they even perched on top of it, seemingly mocking our efforts to scare them.

The monkeys were even braver, and much more destructive than the birds. Unlike the birds, they didn't even eat most of what they picked. A monkey would put an ear of corn under his arm. Then he would see an ear he liked better, so he would drop the first ear and grab the second. Then he would drop the second to grab a third, and so on, until much of the crop had been destroyed.

One day my friends Divane and Albana and I figured out a clever way to trick the monkeys. We caught one of them and put charcoal on it to turn its coat black. Then we let it go back to its group. Apparently, the other monkeys were afraid of it, and they ran, leaving our fields safe—at least for a time.

Keeping birds and monkeys away was a tedious business. I got hot, tired and thirsty. But I did not goof off, because I knew my father would give me a good hiding if I did. Even so, there was one group of invaders I could not keep away no matter how hard I tried—the *mabobo*, or yellow locusts. Whenever they came, we knew we were in for a long, hard, hungry year. We could see them coming from miles away, thousands of them swarming together, turning the sky dark and devouring everything in their path. They could and did strip our fields bare in a matter of minutes. We tried to stop them by swatting at them with stalks of dry grass, but our puny weapons were useless against such vast numbers.

I hated the locusts, not only because they stole our food but because they gave off a terrible stench. I could never understand how other villagers could eat such revolting creatures—but they did.

On the other hand, I saw nothing wrong at all with eating tree worms. They arrived in the spring, their presence announced by the cries of birds in the jungle. These worms showed up just when we had reached our hungriest, and they were often the only things that stood between us and starvation. The worms tasted all right, but one of my favorite treats arrived a little later in the year: termites.

Most Americans and Europeans cannot conceive of eating termites, but they are actually a nutritious, protein-rich food, and many children in Africa eat them. When the time was right for the termites to arrive, the people from my village would gather at night to build a big bonfire to attract them. Pots and pans with water in them were placed in a ditch dug around the fire.

Attracted by the light, the termites would fly toward the fire, only to be overcome by the heat and fall to the ground, right into our ditches. When daylight came, we would emerge to collect our spoils. That was such a happy occasion! It was our version of opening presents on Christmas morning.

We also hunted for rats and mice, which my mother would cut up for stew, by digging in the ground. Although we were delighted to have meat of almost any kind, digging for rats always made me uneasy. One of my uncles lost a finger after being bitten by a snake while he was looking for rodents. His horror story always came to mind when I poked my hand into a hole, probing for something furry that my family could eat.

As a child, I was constantly afraid of dying, and most of my friends shared my fear. And no wonder! We were surrounded by lions, leopards, hyenas, snakes of various kinds, spiders and mosquitoes. And then there were the rival witch doctors and their curses.

Danger was ever crouching at our door—literally. On one occasion, we left our hut in the morning to find a leopard on the limb of a tree right outside. We ran back inside and shut our door, hoping it would be sturdy enough to keep the big cat away if he decided he wanted us for breakfast. My father managed to chase the leopard away by throwing some embers from our fire in its direction. But we were afraid it might come back. Thankfully, it never did.

Wild animals were not the only danger we faced. When the grass grew long and thick, we had to be on our guard for *maphangas*, strangers who were rumored to steal people and sell them as slaves in Malawi. I never saw them, but I was afraid of them just the same. My mother told me they wore big *rastas* and that if anyone fitting this description tried to approach me, I should start shouting for help.

Destined to Be a Witch Doctor?

From the time I was born, my parents hoped I would follow the family tradition and become a witch doctor. I suffered with asthma and other physical ailments, and when my parents sought healing for me, "the spirits" told them that I was sick because I had not given myself over to them. As soon as I had done this, they said, I would be healed.

My family had been involved in witch doctoring for generations. My grandfather kept poisonous snakes to use in rituals and died when one of those snakes bit him. My childhood was full of strange spiritual experiences and spiritual oppression. This was the only life I knew.

My parents did a pretty good business. Every day, people came to the house, many of them weeping, looking for a way out of a desperate situation. Perhaps a child was sick, or the monkeys had stolen their crops. They usually brought a little maize meal or some chicken for my family, but they always had to bring some money, too. My parents would have their "clients" rub the money over their bodies as though washing

23

themselves with soap in the shower. Then they would take the money, put it into a shell and start sniffing it. As they did so they would make a funny noise—"heh, heh, heh"—and then start speaking in a strange tone of voice.

The "advice" that came through was almost always the same, and it played on the person's fears. Someone had put a curse on them. Death was very near. The spirits were angry and had to be appeased. Upon hearing this frightening news, the customers were usually ready to do anything my parents told them to do.

Did my parents have real power, or were they charlatans? The answer is both. Much of what they did was trickery, pure and simple. But I also know that they sincerely believed in the spirits, and I saw many strange events for which I have no other explanation besides the supernatural.

More than once, I found myself floating above the floor as I tried to sleep at night. I struggled and kicked and tried to get back on the ground, but I seemed to be suspended in space. Did it really happen, or was it just a dream? All I can say is that it certainly seemed real to a young boy, and terribly frightening. Later on, when I told my parents about the experience, they became excited and began beating on the drums they used to summon the spirits.

They definitely believed the spirit world was real, but they were not above deceit. As an example of their trickery, they would ask their customer to stare into a bowl full of water until he saw the face of his enemy—the one who had placed a curse on him, his crops or his children. Stirred up by anger and fear, the person would look until he saw someone's face looking back at him—and naturally, the face he saw was the face he expected to see. The neighbor who had given him a strange look. A person he did not like for some reason.

My parents would ask, "Do you want this person to live or die?" By this time, the customer was so agitated that he would almost always say he wanted his enemy to die. He would then be given a stick with a needle attached to the end and be told that he should take revenge on his enemy by striking the image in the water. In most cases, he took the stick and began whacking viciously at the water—which slowly began to turn red. As the water darkened with "blood," the attack would increase in intensity. The customer would slash and cut in the water in a hateful frenzy, literally trying to hack his enemy to pieces.

But there was no blood in that water. The stick that held the needle had been cut from the root of a *mbela* tree, which my parents knew would turn the water red.

Still, there was power in the trickery. Sometimes the enemy would fall sick or even die. I now believe this was due to the faith of my parents' customers. They wanted it to happen so badly that it did.

Every day at sunset, just before the jungle became pitch dark, my mother would go out and pick some of the grass that grew alongside the trails her customers walked each day. Then, she and my father would burn it on the fire in the center of our hut, asking the spirits to give more problems to the people who had walked along these trails. For them, more problems meant more business. The last thing they wanted was for people in the village to be happy and trouble free. Sometimes they would name people and ask the spirits to bring them to our door. The next day, the ones they had named would show up, crying and moaning about the burdens that had fallen on them.

A Life of Misery

As for me, I was oppressed and unhappy, and I cried often. One root of my misery was my sister Maria. I thought Maria was a better person than I was, and I resented her. She was the star of the family, and we both knew it. She was beautiful; she excelled in school. Even though my parents could not read or write, they knew that Maria was a better student than I was. It was easy to tell just by glancing at our schoolwork: Her handwriting was neat and easy to read. My papers looked as if they had been written by a centipede crawling over them.

I was jealous, so I treated her terribly. When we were younger, we often fought, and my father always took her side—which resulted in a severe hiding for me. Once he tied my hands and feet and put me in the hot sun to be bitten by red ants. Fortunately, my mother came along and untied me, after which she and my father got into another terrible fight.

I was also afraid of the strange things I saw and experienced. One day, my friends and I were walking home from school when we came upon a young man walking straight toward us. I thought he would go around us, but instead, he walked right through us. I felt a cold shiver go through me as this ghostly figure seemed to pass through my body. The experience terrified me, but my friends did not even seem to notice.

My parents were no help at all when it came to my fears. Instead, when I told them about frightening things I had seen or sensed, they covered me with a blanket and started beating drums in an effort to get me to allow the spirits to manifest through me. They also beat me with a whip made of horsehair or hit me on my head with a wooden spoon. When I cried out from pain, they beat the drums louder and whipped me harder, because they thought the spirits were beginning to speak through me. I sometimes spent the entire night covered in a blanket, terrified, in pain and praying silently—to whom I did not know—that it would stop.

My mother and father would sing songs over me that were completely meaningless: "The tree of the bird, the lion is sleeping." They sang the same words over and over as they beat their drums. When the situation became almost unbearable, I would start moving around beneath the blanket as if I were not in control of my own body. I knew this would make my parents believe that I was allowing the spirits to take control. This brought relief because my parents would stop whipping me with that horse tail or hitting me with the spoon.

As you can see, my childhood was not a time of happiness and innocence. I was miserable and rarely smiled. My mother often told me, "Don't laugh today or tomorrow you will cry." Even if I had reason to laugh, I would have been afraid to do so. Mine was a life of hopelessness and distress—until the voice woke me up in the dark.

The Adventure Begins

As I slipped out of my home that night, I had no idea where I was going to go.

Then I thought of Gafar, my best friend from school. He was a happy child with a quick smile and a pleasing personality. He was a year older than I, bigger and taller, which meant he would be a good companion on a dangerous journey to who knew where. He loved to talk about anything and everything, and he had a way of getting what he wanted. On the long walk home from school, he often convinced strangers to give us food for the journey, telling them we would die from hunger if they did not help us. His begging skills would prove useful.

I decided to go straight to his house.

His family's hut was about a two-kilometer distance from mine, but as I shuffled along in the darkness, it seemed much farther. I sighed with relief when, at last, I saw it looming just ahead of me.

I waited outside for a few moments, trying to think of a way I could get Gafar's attention without waking the rest of his family. Finally, I decided to call his name and hope for the best.

"Gafar!" I whispered.

No response.

"Gafar!" I tried again, a little louder this time.

Nothing.

"Gafar!"

I heard someone stirring inside and hoped it was not Gafar's father. A few seconds later, my friend appeared in his doorway, wrapped in his sleeping blanket. "What are you doing here?" he asked.

We spoke in hushed tones. "I have to leave," I said, and I told him about the voice and what it had said.

Gafar did not tell me I was crazy or that I should go back home. Instead, he did what I expected him to do. "I'll go with you," he said.

He disappeared into his hut and came back a few minutes later, dressed and with his school bag across his back. Together, we slipped into the jungle.

2

Lost

Although I made a show of being brave, it was frightening to be in the jungle in the middle of the night.

Strange sounds filled the air, as barn owls and other nocturnal animals called out to each other. Insects buzzed around my head. Ferns and other plants slashed at my ankles. More than once, I stumbled over the trunk of a fallen tree. And I began to "see" big cats crouching in every tree.

At first, Gafar and I whispered excitedly to each other.

"Who was it that spoke to you?"

"I don't know. A spirit of great power, I think."

"And you trust him?"

"He was telling me the truth. I'm sure."

"And he told you that you would die . . ."

"If I didn't leave, yes."

Gafar was his usual cheerful self for the first hour or so. But as the night wore on, we both fell silent. I knew he was wondering if he had done the right thing in coming with me, and I was beginning to have second thoughts myself. I had no doubt that I had heard the voice. But could it have been an evil spirit that was trying to trick me? Perhaps the spirit wanted to bring me out here, away from home, to kill me. I felt my mouth and throat go dry.

But the more I thought about it, the more I realized that there was something different about this voice. It had been urgent, yes, but there was a kindness to it as well—a kindness I had never encountered in the spirits that spoke through my parents. I felt certain that the voice meant to save me, not harm me.

Still, I was relieved when I finally saw the huge red ball of the sun rising over the horizon. It seemed to me that the night had lasted for an eternity. The sun brought its own problem, however.

Heat. Scorching, humid heat.

By the time the sun was halfway into the sky, Gafar and I were both drenched in perspiration. I was also exhausted, groggy from lack of sleep.

Suddenly Gafar grabbed my arm and jerked me backward. "Look out!" he shouted, pointing to the ground in front of us.

"What is it?"

"Snake!"

I held my breath and stood completely still. All I could see were the leaves, vines and plants that always seemed to cover the ground in the rain forest.

After a long moment, I relaxed and began breathing again. "Where did it go?" I gasped.

Gafar shook his head. "I don't know. It was right there."

The leaves rustled and a small lizard ran across the path in front of us.

"Maybe it wasn't a snake after all," Gafar admitted. "But it looked like a mamba to me." Despite the hot weather, a chill ran up my spine. "You remember what happened to—" Gafar began.

"Yes, I remember," I interrupted, and I gave him a look that meant, *How could you even ask that question?*

It had been just a year since one of our schoolmates had been bitten by a black mamba. A group of us were walking in the jungle when one of the boys had suddenly cried out in pain. The rest of us immediately ran to his aid—but when we saw the bloody wounds on his leg, and the mamba racing away, we knew there was nothing we could do. The boy wailed in agony and fear as huge tears ran down his face.

Some of the other kids raced back to the village to get his family, while the rest of us stayed with him and told him he was going to be all right, even though we knew it was not true.

By the time the adults from the village reached us, the boy was unconscious. Within half an hour, he was dead.

Gafar and I walked along in silence, haunted by our memories and our fears. We both knew that the rain forest was full of snakes like the black mamba and the even deadlier puff adder. But after a while, our thirst became stronger than our fear.

"Surprise?" Gafar said.

"Yes?"

"We didn't bring any water."

"That's all right," I said cheerfully. "We can get water from the river."

"But what about the crocodiles?"

I shrugged and kept on walking.

Nile crocodiles were common in the lakes and rivers around our village, and they were very good hiders. Often, you could not see them lurking in the water until it was too late. And once those powerful jaws grabbed hold of you, there was nothing you could do. I shuddered at the thought.

After a few more hours of walking in the hot sun, Gafar and I both began to think we had made a terrible mistake. We had nothing to eat. Mosquitoes and gnats pestered us constantly. And the sun beat down on us relentlessly.

Finally, we decided to sit down, rest and take stock of our situation.

"Let's Go Home"

After a few minutes Gafar spoke. "I think we should go home," he said. He sounded a bit defensive, as if he expected an argument from me. He did not get one.

"Yes." I nodded. "We should go home."

"But what about the voice?" he asked.

"The voice told me to leave, and I did," I answered. "Perhaps it's safe to return now."

Relief showed in Gafar's eyes. "Let me rest for a bit," he said. We fell silent, and within minutes we were both asleep.

When I woke up, the sun was high in the sky but heading toward the western horizon. We had to start moving if we were to get home before dark. I did not want to spend another night in the jungle. Gafar was awake, too, and I could tell he was thinking the same thing.

We rose and dusted ourselves off. Even though I was used to going without food, my stomach was burning with hunger. Before I did anything else, I had to find something to eat. By God's grace, it did not take long to find a mango tree with several round, yellow fruits hanging from its branches. Gafar and I grabbed mangoes with both hands and began gobbling them down. I thought they were the best mangoes I had ever tasted. If I had known how many of them I was going to eat over the next two weeks, I would not have been so enthusiastic.

Fortified by our mango meal, my companion and I headed back the way we had come. Both of us agreed about which way we should go. Neither of us doubted that we were headed in the right direction. We walked until the sun began to sink, and we still had not come to the narrow dirt path that led directly to our village.

"We'll be home before dark," I said, trying to convince myself. "We'll come upon the path any time now."

"Of course." Gafar grinned. "We're almost home."

But it was not so. Rather, it was as if the path back to our village had completely disappeared. Becoming disoriented in the jungle is easy to do. The trees, vines and other plants are so thick that they become like a huge maze. There are no distinguishing landmarks, and everything begins to look the same. We were hopelessly lost.

We passed a tree that looked familiar. Surely we had been through here earlier today? I was certain that I recognized that vine, this flowering shrub. What was going on? We were walking in a straight line, so why was it that we seemed to be going in circles?

I still do not know the answer.

Gafar and I spent the next two weeks wandering in the jungle. I ate mangoes until I could barely stand the sight of them. Thankfully, the jungle was full of other food as well. We found wild bananas and an occasional yam or other tuber. We ate termites, beetles, grubs and other insects. Because we had grown up on the edge of the rain forest, we knew to stay away from brightly colored bugs, or those with stingers. We also knew to avoid plants that had white or yellow berries, that had leaves in groups of three, or that were protected by thorns. As for mushrooms, we avoided them altogether. We knew that some mushrooms were deadly, and there was no point in taking a chance.

We drank water wherever we could find it. We scooped it out of mud holes with our bare hands. In the morning, we sipped the dew that collected on the leaves of plants on the jungle floor. Some plants produced a few drops of water when we twisted and squeezed them like a sponge. But this was hardly enough to quench our thirst.

A River We Had to Cross

We knew there was a major river nearby, but we never saw it.

To me, that remains one of the great mysteries of our journey. Years later, when I used a map to trace the journey

Gafar and I had taken, it clearly showed that we had to cross the Shire River at some point. The Shire is one of the major tributaries of the Zambezi, and it is seldom narrower than fifty meters wide.

But we never saw it. I cannot explain how this happened, but I know it did.

At night, we often slept in trees, tying ourselves to the branches to keep from falling out. We figured it was better to risk falling out of a tree than to sleep on the ground and risk being killed by a wild animal, bitten by a poisonous snake or stung to death by a horde of army ants.

It still amazes me that neither of us was seriously injured or became ill. Malaria was a danger; it is a terrible problem in Mozambique, killing thousands of children every year. Gafar and I were pestered constantly by mosquitoes and bitten many times, but neither one of us got so much as a mild case of fever. Nor did we become ill from drinking dirty water. The water we drank had to be teeming with bacteria and intestinal parasites, but we suffered no ill effects. Surely God had His hand on us.

The worst part of the journey was being lost. I missed my family and even my sister Maria. I wondered what had happened to them, if they were alive and looking for me. I also worried that Gafar and I would spend the rest of our lives in the wilderness, without another living person to talk to. When I had first realized we were lost, I had been afraid. Very quickly, fear was replaced by loneliness—a loneliness that was deep, dark and overwhelming.

A New Beginning

Then, on the fourteenth day of our journey, late in the afternoon, I saw something in the distance. "Look!" I shouted to Gafar, pointing toward a clearing in the jungle a few hundred meters distant.

"Houses!" he cried. "People!" We began running as fast as we could.

Our wanderings had taken us all the way across Mozambique's Tete Province to the town of Vila Nova da Fronteira, on the border of Malawi. As we stumbled out of the jungle, we were surprised to see an elderly man standing at the edge of the clearing. His white beard and bushy white hair made him look like a wild man. But a friendly grin spread across his face when he saw us, and he raised his hand in greeting.

"I'm glad you're finally here, boys," he called out to us. "I've been waiting for you."

3

I Saw You in a Dream

The old man was not much to look at, with his wrinkled, weather-beaten face and shaggy, unkempt hair. And yet, whoever he was, I had never been so glad to see another human being. No angel could have seemed more beautiful at that moment.

He smiled broadly as he strode toward us. "Welcome, boys! Welcome!" A joyful light seemed to shine in his eyes. His face may have been old and weathered, but those eyes were alive with fire and life. Somehow I knew he was a good man and that we could trust him completely.

"You boys need something to eat," he laughed. "And a good night's sleep."

I glanced at Gafar and wondered if I looked as disgusting as he did. We had tried to keep clean, without much success. I noticed for the first time that my friend's hair was matted with dirt, grass and twigs. His clothes were ragged and filthy, his arms and legs caked with mud. I noticed something else, too: He smelled terrible. We both did. In our village, when something had a bad odor, we always said it smelled "like an old snake." Gafar and I smelled like old snakes.

Our new friend, who said his name was Mr. Lukas, seemed unaware of our old-snake aroma. "Come along," he said, as he turned and headed toward the town. "My house is only a short walk from here."

In Africa, where people are accustomed to traveling on foot, a short walk may mean a distance up to several kilometers. Gafar and I were so tired that we fell into step beside him without asking questions. Wherever he was taking us, no matter how far, it had to be better than spending another night in the jungle.

Vila Nova is a small village of a few hundred people. Some of the houses were built of reeds, mud and thatch, like the ones in my village. Others were constructed of cement blocks or wood, and though I realize now that many of them were barely more than shacks, they seemed very fancy to me. It was late afternoon and the streets were empty and quiet, which made the whole situation seem like a dream.

Thankfully, after just ten minutes, we came to a small mud and thatch house. A dozen or so chickens scratched around in the yard, looking for tasty bugs. Mr. Lukas stopped and gestured for us to go on in.

As we walked through the door we were met by a small white-haired woman—apparently our host's wife. Her eyes widened in surprise when she saw us, and she instinctively backed away—probably due to our old-snake smell.

"We have visitors," her husband announced, giving the news just a little late. He may have known we were coming, but it was clear that his wife had not.

I am certain we looked as if we had just crawled out of the jungle, which of course we had. My shirt, which had been purple when we started, was now dirty brown. My trousers were the same color. Gafar's once-white shirt bore no resemblance to its former self. We stared at each other for a moment, neither of us quite knowing what to do.

Suddenly, the woman nodded, and a smile spread across her face. "Welcome to our home," she said.

"These are the young men I told you about," her husband explained. "They have been in the jungle for some time." I wondered how he could have told her about us when we had just met him.

"Yes, I see," his wife responded. "I'll heat some water so you can take a shower."

She pointed in the direction of the outside thatch bathroom, where she and her husband showered and relieved themselves. I suppose that by western standards the place was disgusting. The best way I can describe it is that it was like taking a shower in a foul-smelling outhouse. That did not matter to us. We were thrilled to rinse off the old-snake odor, and we emerged feeling refreshed and hopeful.

We took in our new surroundings. The Lukases' home consisted of two small huts, one of them with a sleeping area. The other hut had a cooking pit in the center and served as a refuge for the chickens when it rained. As we entered the small home again, the aroma of fish and sweet potato awaited us, and sleeping mats had been spread on the floor. I had never tasted a meal so delicious! Gafar and I ate like starving men, shoving the food down as if we feared it was about to jump off our plates and run away. This was so much better than the roots and plants we had been eating for the past few days.

Our hosts waited on us as if we were their own children. They did not ask any questions about who we were or why we had been in the jungle; their only concern seemed to be tending to our needs.

As soon as we had eaten our fill, we lay down on the mats and I was quickly asleep. It was the first night since we had left home that I was able to lie down without fear. I slept deeply all night long.

The next morning Gafar and I awoke to a bright, crisp day. The sky above was a deep, clear blue, without a single cloud. We found Mr. Lukas outside, sitting on a small wooden chair in the shade of a tall, dark thorn tree, eating a breakfast of stone-baked sweet potatoes.

He called out to us. "Boys! Come have something to eat." He gestured to a couple of mats that were unrolled over the ground. The orange flesh of the sweet potato looked delicious, and we hurried over to join him.

As we began to eat I asked the question that had been on my mind from the moment we had emerged from the jungle. "Mr. Lukas," I said, "you told us that you were waiting for us. How could you know we were coming when we ourselves didn't know?"

"That's right," Gafar chimed in. "We have been lost in the jungle for days."

Mr. Lukas nodded and chuckled softly. "I saw you in a dream," he said.

"I see," I said. This was not terribly surprising news. I believed that such things happened and thought that Mr. Lukas must be a witch doctor, like my parents. And yet I had not seen anything in his house to make me believe this was true: no mysterious drawings or symbols, no collection of magical herbs, no ritual drums.

"A dream?" Gafar asked, before shoving another huge piece of sweet potato into his mouth.

"Yes. God showed me in a dream that you were coming. He told me to go to the edge of the jungle and wait for two boys who were hungry and exhausted. He also told me to take care of you when you arrived."

I had expected him to say that the revelation had come from a spirit—not from God. Furthermore, I was not sure which god he was talking about. I had grown up believing in many gods and spirits who had to be appeased constantly. I also believed that there was a "great God," but He was far away and could not be expected to care about the daily struggles of human beings.

Learning about God

Before I had a chance to ask Mr. Lukas which god he was referring to, he leaned back in his chair and began a story:

"In the beginning, God created everything we see—the sky, the earth and the trees. He created all the animals and people. And it was only when He made people that He exerted Himself."

I put down my cup of water while Gafar paused in his chewing. We listened in silence as he went on, his booming voice echoing in our ears.

"God did not exert Himself when He made the elephant," he explained. "He did not exert Himself making the lion. He did not exert Himself making the rivers. He did not exert Himself making the great oceans, the little animals or the birds. It was only when He made the first man and woman that He exerted Himself and invested His strength."

He paused for a moment to let that sink in. "The creation of human beings was God's greatest achievement. He poured Himself into us, creating us in His own image. This is why God loves us so much. He wants only the best for us. But some people chose to obey His enemy, Satan, the evil one. That's why God sent His Son, Jesus. He came to earth in human form, just like you and me."

That was the first time in my life that I had heard the name *Jesus*.

"What happened then?" I asked.

"Jesus told the people about God's love," he said. "He healed the sick. He raised the dead. He said, 'Love your enemies and do good to all people.' But some would not listen to Him. They continued in their evil ways. They did this even though God had sent His Son—His only Son—into the world so that He could save us from our sin, so that we can go to heaven and live with God forever after we die."

Mr. Lukas reached out to put his hand on my shoulder. "God gave us a choice. You can follow Jesus and go to heaven, or you can follow Satan, the evil one, and he will take you to hell."

I did not know what hell was, but I could tell from the way he said the word that it was a horrible place, and I did not want to go there.

Mr. Lukas's eyes were aflame with passion; he seemed to be looking into my soul. "Many chose to follow Satan and go to hell. In fact, they killed Jesus."

Gafar and I both gasped at this terrible news.

"They beat Him and nailed Him to a tree," he explained. "Then they laughed at Him as they watched Him die."

"No!" I cried. That the Son of God should have been treated so horribly made me sick at heart. I felt a pain within my chest, and tears began to bubble up from deep inside me. I had not shed a single tear the night the voice told me to leave my family behind. But now I felt as if my best friend had died. What made it worse was that somehow I knew that *I* was as guilty as those who had nailed Him to the tree. I felt that I had spent my whole life following Satan—I was destined for hell.

I closed my eyes, blinking back tears as Mr. Lukas went on to explain how Jesus had forgiven those who treated Him so horribly. This amazed me; Jesus was so different from the spirits my parents wanted me to serve.

I also immediately grasped that everything Mr. Lukas was telling us was true. The fifteen years of my life that I had not served the Lord felt like a waste. Then, the truth had been hidden from me; now, I felt great relief because the truth had been revealed before my eyes.

He talked about how Jesus had been raised from the dead on the third day after His death and how He had ascended into heaven. Then Mr. Lukas began to describe the horrors that awaited those who turned their backs on Jesus. In my mind I could see the fires of hell burning as if the flames had materialized before me. I saw myself on a precipice, about to plunge into hell, with boiling water beneath me and roaring flames all about. I could almost feel the heat on my skin.

Shaking and crying, I fell to my knees and grabbed Mr. Lukas's hands. "Please, help me!" I begged. "I want to follow Jesus. Tell me what to do."

Mr. Lukas put his hands on my shoulders. "Do you believe that Jesus is the Christ, the Son of the living God?" he thundered.

"Yes!"

"Do you accept Him as your Lord and Savior?"

"Yes—of course!"

"Do you believe that He took your sins upon Himself and died on your behalf?"

"Yes, I do."

As we knelt on that straw mat in the shade of the thorn tree, Mr. Lukas led me—and then Gafar—in the sinner's prayer. I knew I was in the presence of the great God, Creator of the earth and everything in it.

By the time we said, "Amen," I felt like a volcano had erupted in my soul. The tears streaming down my cheeks were now tears of joy. I felt the same exhilaration I had known as a boy when I sat alone at night, looking at the star-filled sky.

Mr. Lukas said, "Now you are children of God. You are on the way to heaven, and Jesus will always hold your hand." At that moment, happiness entered my life; joy filled my heart; fire ignited in my spirit. It seemed as though something that had been pressing on my chest had been released, and now I could breathe again.

A Glimpse of Heaven

That night, sleeping once again on Mr. Lukas's floor, I dreamed I was in heaven.

I walked down golden streets surrounded by pearly white mansions far more beautiful than I could hope to describe. Their roofs were made of precious stones and their doors of diamonds. They had freshly mowed lawns of lush, green grass. Keep in mind that I had never seen a mansion before, and nobody in my village had a lawn. So my dream was not based on a memory of something I had experienced.

I saw brightly colored birds flying in formation with their wings touching each other. They knew my name and welcomed me in my native language. Everything was so neat and clear, so bright and shiny. Everything was good.

The joy and peace of that dream remained when I woke up the next morning. Even now, when I think about it, I cannot help but smile.

Gafar and I spent the next five weeks with Mr. and Mrs. Lukas. Every morning we had breakfast under the thorn tree, and then we went off to help them in their maize and cassava fields, which they tended by hand. We worked long, hard hours. It was almost like being home. In the evening Mrs. Lukas always prepared a tasty meal for us, and then we would sleep on their floor.

Mr. Lukas could not stop talking about Jesus, and that made me happy. I hung on every word he said. His wife was quiet, probably because her husband did not stop talking long enough for her to say very much, but I could tell she was a strong person. She, too, loved Jesus with all her heart.

About a week after arriving in Vila Nova, Gafar and I went to the Shire River to try to catch some fish for dinner. There, I struck up a conversation with some men who made their living on the water.

"Have you ever been to Cachote?" I asked.

One of them nodded. "A few days ago." He shook his head as if the memory were painful.

"That's my home," I said.

"But you haven't been there recently. Am I right?"

"No, I haven't. Why?"

"Terrible things there. People have been killed."

A lump formed in my throat. "Killed? Who? How?"

"I don't know. But it's very bad."

I knew immediately that my parents were dead, although it was not until several years later that I learned they had been poisoned by rival witch doctors. My heart broke to hear this terrible news. The thought of my poor mother lying cold and lifeless was almost more than I could bear. At that moment, more than at any other time in my life, I realized how much I loved her.

Immediately, I felt God's loving arms wrap around me, comforting me and sustaining me during this time of loss. Still, I felt so guilty. Why was I saved? And why had I not warned my family? How I wished I had awakened them and asked them to come with me!

Of all my family, God chose me—but why?

4

Loaves and Fishes

I will never forget the time Gafar and I spent with Mr. and Mrs. Lukas. For me it was, I suppose, like the three years Paul spent in the desert after encountering Christ on the road to Damascus. Through this kind spiritual guide and his wife, the Lord was preparing me for service in His Kingdom.

Then one night, Gafar came to me and told me he thought it was time for us to move on. I was surprised, because I had always been the leader and Gafar the follower. Not this time; Gafar was right. The voice had not called me out of my home in the middle of the night only to have me spend the rest of my life working in the Lukases' fields and sleeping on their floor. God had a greater purpose for me, and I now knew that I was to give my life in service to Jesus Christ.

"Where should we go?" Gafar asked.

"I don't know," I admitted. "Wherever God leads."

"Malawi?" he asked.

"Yes, perhaps Malawi," I answered.

I had never been to Malawi, and the thought excited me, although it also made me nervous. I did not know much about Malawi or what language its people spoke. I had grown up speaking the Shona language, which is widespread in much of southern Africa. In school, I had also learned to speak Portuguese, the national language of Mozambique. So I figured that I would at least be able to communicate. Besides, if God was behind our talk of moving to Malawi, this could be the beginning of a great new adventure.

The next morning, Gafar and I thanked Mr. and Mrs. Lukas for their hospitality, spent some time in prayer with them and then set out on foot. We had no idea where we were headed, but we knew that God was guiding us, and He would let us know when we had reached our destination.

We walked for days, deep into Malawi, talking about Jesus to everyone we met. This journey was far different from our time in the Mozambican jungle. There Gafar and I had often been so frightened that our hair stood straight up on our heads. In Malawi, we walked through miles of grassland and slept in cultivated fields at night. We felt perfectly safe.

Sometimes, as darkness began to fall, we went to a farmhouse or village and explained that we were passing through and needed a place to sleep. Every time the families we approached shared their food with us and invited us to sleep on their floor. There was no suspicion and no selfishness. Some of these people had almost nothing, but they were willing to share the little they had.

One evening, just outside a village called Ngabu, we were just bedding down for the night when we heard what sounded like a shrill, high-pitched laugh far in the distance. Then another, a bit louder—a bit closer. "Hyenas!" Gafar gasped.

Now, the hyena may have a cry that sounds like laughter, but he is not the least bit funny. He is a vicious animal with sharp teeth and even sharper claws. I had heard stories about packs of hyenas killing people, and I did not doubt them. I had also heard that hyenas were in league with demons and evil spirits, and even though I knew I was protected by the blood of Jesus, I did not like the sound of that crazy laugh.

There it was again, a bit nearer than before.

"Ha ha ha ha hoo hoo ha ha!"

"It's closer," I said. "We had better find a safe place to stay."

"Ha ha ha ha hoo hoo hee hee!"

Not too far down the road, we came upon a mud and thatch house. The young couple who lived there warmly welcomed us to their home. It turned out they were believers, and we had a wonderful time of fellowship with them. The couple shared with us their meager dinner, which consisted primarily of millet from their fields and a thick porridge called *nsima*, which is made of maize flour. What a treat it was to have a hot meal, even though there was not quite enough to fill my stomach! Our hosts were warm, friendly and ready to share whatever they had—which is typical of so many people I have encountered during my travels through rural Africa.

When our meal was finished, we sat around the fire, and our host asked us where we were going. "We don't know for certain," we told him.

"Go to a city called Nchalo. There is a sugar plantation there, with many jobs."

"How long will it take us to get there?" Gafar asked.

Our host scratched his head as he thought about it. "It is eight . . . perhaps nine days' journey."

We headed in the direction of Nchalo the very next morning, promising to be careful and to keep our eyes open for danger. By the grace of God, the remainder of our journey was free from encounters with hyenas or other predators. But when we finally reached the sugar plantation ten days later, we were disappointed to discover that we were not old enough to be hired.

What Now, Lord?

Our shoulders were drooping as we walked along the road leading out of town. As the sun sank below the distant horizon, I began to pray out loud: "Lord, please show us what You want us to do. You know that we want to serve You, and we're willing to go anywhere or do anything. We just need You to show us the way. Thank You, Jesus."

Almost immediately, we heard the joyful sound of voices lifted together in song. We stopped to listen. People were singing about Jesus! We ran in the direction of the sound until we stopped in front of a small white building. A sign in front proclaimed *Church of God of Prophecy*.

We hurried inside, finding perhaps a hundred people sitting on wooden pews, clapping their hands as they loudly sang songs of praise to God. Heads turned and faces smiled in welcome. We were many miles from home, and in a foreign country, but we were among family. Gafar and I sat on the back row and joined in the worship, even though we had never heard the song before.

Before the service was over that night, I found myself standing in front of the little congregation, telling them what God was doing in my life. Amidst shouts of "Hallelujah!" and "Praise the Lord!" I told how God had called to me in the middle of the night, about the two weeks Gafar and I wandered lost in the jungle and how Mr. Lukas had led us into a relationship with Jesus Christ.

That was the first time I had ever spoken in front of a group of any size, but I felt completely at ease. When the pastor invited me to share my testimony, I was a bit nervous at first, but as soon as I opened my mouth, it seemed as if God Himself was speaking through me. I now know that I was experiencing what Jesus described to His disciples:

On my account you will be brought before governors and kings as witnesses to them and to the Gentiles. But . . . do

50

not worry about what to say or how to say it. At that time you will be given what to say, for it will not be you speaking, but the Spirit of your Father speaking through you.

Matthew 10:18–20

This kind of supernatural occurrence was actually not unusual for me. Since the day I surrendered my life to the Lord, I had been having dreams about God and heaven almost every night, and I was also seeing visions in the day. In fact, I was so absorbed by the spiritual realm that at times I was not sure whether I was in the spiritual world or the physical one. Sometimes I thought I was dreaming, only to discover that I was actually talking to someone. As I talked in the little church that night, it was almost as if I were standing off to the side, listening to myself as the Holy Spirit spoke through me.

When the service was over, Gafar and I were approached by a man and his wife, Silva and Basi. Knowing that we had no place to stay, they invited us to come home with them. It turned out that Silva owned a brick factory in the area, and Gafar and I spent the next three months working for him. Once again, God intervened to meet our needs. We quickly grew to love Silva and Basi, and we learned much from them as we saw them demonstrate God's love in their marriage and their business.

During the three months we spent making bricks, Gafar and I attended the little church every time the doors were open. We were a couple of wide-eyed children, hearing those amazing Bible stories for the first time. We laughed in amazement as we learned how God parted the Red Sea so the Israelites could escape from the pursuing Egyptian army. We held our breath as the pastor told of the little shepherd boy, David, going out to battle the fierce giant Goliath. And we hung our heads in sorrow as we heard how the apostle Peter denied Christ three times after promising that he was willing to die for Him.

After three months had passed, Silva and Basi sent us to work in some fields they owned on a remote island called Chikusi, in the middle of the Shire River. When we got there, we were disappointed to find out there was no church in the area. So we decided to make our own. We went door to door, inviting everyone to a church service that evening. I also invited everyone I encountered while in the fields.

Eight people showed up. We stood around the fire we had made to keep the mosquitoes at bay, and Gafar and I sang some of the songs we had learned in the little church in Nchalo. I was inexperienced and awkward, but I was also available. And, as I have seen many times, God will use anyone who is willing and available.

As I began to preach, I suddenly felt as if my heart would break. Love and compassion for these dear people flooded through me. I know now that I was seeing them the way God does. Some of them had lost children to disease and hunger. They were sick and hungry themselves. They did not know what they were going to feed their families tomorrow. Some owned only the clothes they wore—nothing else.

Even worse, they did not know they had a heavenly Father who loved them dearly, who sent His Son to save them.

In reality I was probably as poor as they were when it came to worldly possessions. But I had Jesus, and that made all the difference. At the same time I still did not know much about the Bible and did not have a copy of my own.

There was one other major drawback: I did not speak their language.

Somehow they had understood that we were going to have a meeting that night, but that was about it. They recognized a few words of my language, and I knew a few words of theirs, but we did not know enough for real communication to take place. I discovered this as soon as I launched into my best impression of the pastor I had heard so often in Nchalo.

Looking into the open, earnest faces of the little congregation, I began, "God has a destiny for each and every one of you."

Blank faces looked back at me.

"That destiny is in His Son, Jesus," I continued.

Nothing.

Gafar, who was standing next to me, leaned closer and whispered what I already knew: "They don't understand."

He was right, of course, but the only thing I could do at this point was keep going. *Lord*, I prayed silently, *please help me find a way to tell these people about Your love.*

I cleared my throat and started over. "Jesus Christ came from heaven to save us from our sins." I glanced around to see if I could detect a flicker of understanding. Finding none, I decided to go ahead and preach my sermon anyway.

"Some people are rebelling against Jesus," I said. "Those people will go to hell because they have rejected the One who came to save us from our sins."

I cannot tell you the exact moment it happened, but as I continued, I was suddenly aware that I was no longer speaking in my own language. Gafar's eyes grew wide, as if he thought I had lost my mind and was spouting gibberish. I think we both realized at the same instant that I was speaking the local Chichewa dialect. It was as if someone had thrown a switch and everyone was immediately able to understand me.

From that day forward, I have been able to speak the Chichewa language fluently. In fact, the very first Bible I ever owned was in the Chichewa language. This was the first of many occasions when God supernaturally enabled me to speak a language I had never learned.

The small group of five women and three men sat transfixed as I told them about the great love of Jesus, who had given His own life for us that we might live forever in heaven with God. I described heaven in vivid detail, excitement rising in me as I recalled the beautiful dream God had given me the night after I surrendered my life to Christ.

I concluded by asking everyone who wanted to commit their lives to Jesus to kneel down. Everyone knelt.

Now what?

I was not quite sure what I was supposed to do next. Then I remembered how Mr. Lukas had put his hands on our heads and prayed for us when Gafar and I had accepted Christ. I went down the line, laying my hands on every head and praying for God to bless and nurture His children.

Such joy filled our hearts that night! Everyone joined in a celebration that continued well into the night—singing, dancing and laughing before the Lord.

That was the beginning of a church that meets in Chikusi until this very day. And although I had no way of knowing it, that little congregation was the first of more than ten thousand churches God would use me to plant in Malawi, Mozambique and throughout southern Africa.

5

Signs and Wonders

The joy and excitement of experiencing God's presence in such a powerful way was still with me the next day as I went out to work in the fields. I was eagerly looking forward to another meeting that evening.

Late in the afternoon, just as daylight was beginning to fade, I heard someone scream in the distance. I stopped working and scanned the maize fields.

Over there! A woman was sobbing as if in terrible pain, and someone else was shouting my name. "Surprise! Surprise!"

In the last glimmers of sunlight, I could make out a small knot of people headed in my direction. As they drew closer, I saw that a young woman in the middle of the group had been seriously injured in some way. Although she was supported by four other workers, she was stumbling and staggering as they came toward me. She sobbed in pain as she cried, "I don't want to die! Oh, God! Please don't let me die."

I dropped my hoe and ran to them.

The injured woman was just a girl, really, no more than twenty years old and wearing the simple *kaplana* cloth tied below her shoulders. I saw at a glance that her right leg was already swollen to twice the size of the left one, and someone had used a shirt as a makeshift tourniquet. Tears of pain and fear streamed down her face.

I recognized some of those with her from the previous night's meeting. "What happened?" I asked.

"Snakebite," one of them gasped. "A puff adder," added another.

"She must go to the clinic!" a man insisted. One of the women shook her head. "It's too far. She won't make it." She put her hand on my shoulder. "Will Jesus make her well?"

It had never occurred to me that Jesus could and would heal the sick. But I knew He could do anything He wanted to do—and unless He helped her, this poor girl *was* going to die. I sat down beside her and put my hands on her swollen leg. I had no idea what words to use, so I simply began praying. "Bless Your child. Bless Your child. Lord Jesus, please bless Your child." I said the words over and over again, and as I prayed small droplets of water began to drain out of her injured leg. At first I thought she was sweating, but a moment later the fluid was gushing out, returning the leg to its normal size.

The crowd gasped.

The woman stopped crying and wiped the tears from her face. "It doesn't hurt anymore!" she shouted. "The pain is gone."

"Are you certain?" I asked her.

"Yes, I am!" Her eyes were red, but there were no tears.

"Stand up and see if you can walk," I urged her.

She stood up, and we were amazed to see her walking easily, without even a slight limp. After a few steps she turned to me with a huge smile on her face and said, "It feels fine."

Suddenly everyone was pushing in, talking excitedly and wanting to know more about Jesus. That night our meeting was full of people who had heard about the miracle and wanted to know more about the Lord.

Back in the fields the next day, the first thing I did was find the woman who had been bitten by the snake. "How are you today?" I asked.

"Very good." She smiled.

"Does your leg hurt?"

"Not at all," she assured me. Then she told me that when she had gone to bed the night before, she began to feel afraid that she would die during the night. But she had slept well and awoke feeling fine, and now she knew for certain that she had been healed.

Over the next few days and weeks our little church grew rapidly. Gafar and I were utterly on fire for Jesus, and we talked about Him wherever we went. Because I could not bear the thought of anyone going into the fire of hell, I felt compelled to share the Gospel with as many people as I could. Sometimes I lay awake at night, grieving over the lost souls who were all around me.

A Glimpse of Hell

When I was not at work or leading worship, I sometimes went into town and rode the bus for an hour or two, just so I could talk to my fellow passengers about Jesus. One day I was on a crowded bus when the floor seemed to crumble away, and I saw that we were suspended over a deep chasm full of fire. I heard flames crackling beneath us and felt their heat on my face. It was so real to me that I did not know it was a vision.

Panic-stricken, I tried to shout a warning to the woman who sat across from me. I felt that if she did not hold on for dear life, she would go tumbling into the flames. People all around me were in horrible danger, but they were completely unaware of this. They were talking, laughing and reading their books as if everything were perfectly fine. They had no idea of the horror that awaited them.

As quickly as it came the vision evaporated and the floor of the bus came back together. I sat rooted to my seat, shaking from fear. Even though the vision had ended, I knew the danger and the horror were real.

Many times since then I have had similar visions of the earth opening up and people falling into hell. This is why I have always been determined to do everything I can to keep people from going to that terrible place. It is also one reason why our little group grew so quickly.

Another reason was that we were seeing God confirm His Word with miracles: healing the sick, setting people free from demonic bondage and making Himself known in many other ways. One evening a woman asked for prayer because she was in terrible pain from a toothache; she was instantly healed through prayer. Another time we watched in awe as a cancerous tumor withered away under the power of Jesus' name. Another person was healed of yellow fever.

Within five or six weeks our little church had grown to an average attendance of about sixty people. Things were going well, and I could see myself spending the rest of my life in Chikusi, except for one thing: I had a growing feeling that God wanted me to share the Gospel with even more people who were lost and on their way to hell. I felt compelled to reach out to the world beyond Chikusi. And how could I reach the world if I stayed in one place?

The thought of journeying across Africa to share the Gospel with as many people as possible thrilled me. Nothing in the world made me feel as good as when I led a sinner in the prayer of salvation.

While I felt God was calling me on to new adventures, I did not realize that Gafar was also feeling that it was time for a change, nor did I anticipate where God was calling him to go.

We were walking home one night when I noticed that he was unusually thoughtful and quiet. "Okay," I finally prodded him. "What is it?"

"What is what?"

I put my hand on his shoulder. "You're acting strange. What's on your mind?" He laughed, and then we walked along for a while in silence.

"Listen, brother," I said at last, putting my arm around his shoulder. "Either you're sick or something is bothering you. Which is it?"

He sighed. "It's just that . . . I've been thinking that perhaps I should go back to Mozambique."

He caught me completely by surprise. I did not know what to say. "What do you think?" he asked.

I forced a smile and answered, "You have to do what you want to do."

"No." He shook his head. "I have to do what God wants me to do."

"Amen!" I laughed. I knew better than to argue with that.

Gafar explained that he felt God was calling him back to Vila Nova to help Mr. Lukas share the Gospel there. It was surprising because he was the one who first felt that God was calling us away from there. He asked me if I wanted to go with him, but I could not, for two reasons. First of all, everything I had known there was gone; Mozambique was no longer home to me, for there was nothing to return to.

More importantly, I knew that it was not where God was calling me to go. I felt certain that He wanted me to resume traveling across Malawi, telling lost souls about the love of Jesus.

Sharing a Message from God

It took a few days for us to prepare to leave. We wanted to be sure we were leaving the church in good hands, and we also did not want to leave without giving Silva and Basi ample warning. Soon enough, the time came for us to hug each other good-bye, and we headed in opposite directions.

As I waved farewell to the many friends from church who had come to see us off, a homesick feeling swept over me. In only a few weeks these dear people had become my family, and now I was losing them. It was the same feeling I had had when Gafar and I decided to tell Mr. and Mrs. Lukas good-bye. It would have been easy to stay on this island and start building a life there. But I knew for certain there was something more for me to do. I could not stay on the ground while God was telling me to reach for the stars.

I walked along a narrow black-topped road that meandered over gently rolling hills. I did not really know where I was going, but that did not matter to me. I knew God was guiding my steps, and I was ready to go anywhere He wanted me to go.

Even though Gafar had been my constant companion for several months, I did not feel the least bit lonely. Jesus was with me and my heavenly Father was watching over me, so I walked along with a huge smile on my face. That morning my only concern was for those who did not know the love of Christ.

I also had plenty of company. Africans are accustomed to walking long distances every day, and in many areas the roadsides are crowded with pedestrians. As I walked along, young girls in colorful dresses passed by with heavy buckets full of water balanced on their heads. Men on bicycles zigzagged in and out of traffic, as did goats, sheep and other animals. A man hurried past, pushing a wheelbarrow full of bricks. A couple of young boys proudly displayed the field mice they had caught; their mother would have meat for her stew tonight.

It was a beautiful day, with the morning sun high in a bright blue sky. Walking in Africa can be a dangerous business, however; cars whizzed past, so close to me that my trouser legs fluttered in the breeze. Drivers occasionally honked their horns, but, as is typical in rural Africa, no one ever slowed down.

After an hour or so I came to a dirt road curving to the right of the highway. A wooden sign listed several villages with the distance to each. I sensed immediately that God's heart was breaking for many of the people who lived in these villages. Many of them had never had a chance to hear the Gospel. If I did not share God's love with them, who would? I headed down the dirt road, my sandals kicking up small plumes of dust in my wake. Once in a while a lizard scurried out of the bush and scrambled across the road in front of me. It was good being off the highway.

Before long I came to a mud and thatch hut; nearby a couple of chickens scratched in the dirt. I was nearing the first village.

I decided that I would go either to the local market or to the community's water source. At either of those locations, I would almost certainly find a few people engaged in conversation, and I could tell them about Jesus. As I drew nearer to the small village, the sound of women's laughter floated on the air. Following the happy noise, I soon came to a small well where half a dozen women were filling their families' water jars. They were relishing the latest gossip and news together.

"*Mwauka bwanji* [Good morning]," I called out, lifting my hand in what I hoped was a friendly greeting.

The happy conversation fell silent and all of the women turned their heads in my direction. "*Mwauka bwanji,*" one of the older women called back. Her voice was strong and firm, and I figured she was the "leader" of this small gathering. These women probably did not see many strangers in their village. Even so, their smiling faces showed no hint of fear or suspicion. Of course I was only a boy, still not quite sixteen years old. Two or three of them probably had children my age, and that helped open the door for me.

"I have an important message for your village," I said, addressing the woman who had spoken to me.

"Message? From who?" she demanded.

61

"From God."

"God?"

"Yes. He wants you to know that He loves you very much."

"Are you talking to me?"

"Yes." I nodded and swept my hand from left to right. "I'm talking to all of you."

The grandmother of the group cupped her hands to her mouth and let out a whoop of laughter, as if the thought that God loved her was the silliest thing she had ever heard. The other women laughed with her, but they were still intrigued. *What in the world could this young stranger be up to?* They were not gullible children after all; they would not be taken in by any fast-talking stranger with something to sell. But they wanted to hear more.

Their caution was not because they did not respect God; most tribal people in sub-Saharan Africa believe in a great creator God. They just do not believe He cares about people. Their reasoning is that He is too great and we are too insignificant. Why should He care? He has more important things to do than get involved in the lives of human beings.

"God loves you so much that He gave His Son to die for you," I said. "He will forgive you of everything you've ever done that was wrong, and He will give you eternal life."

The spokeswoman of the group gestured at a large rock on the edge of the stream. "Sit down," she invited. "We want to hear more." They listened with rapt attention as I shared the Gospel with them. Before we were finished, every one of them had prayed to receive Christ as Lord and Savior.

Then they took me to the chief's house, where I was granted permission to hold a service in the middle of the village that night. I knew that if I had the chief's backing, people would come to hear me—and they did. The village was small, perhaps 300 people, including the babies and children. We all gathered in a small field where the children had just concluded a game of football (what Americans call *soccer*). A man brought me one of his treasured possessions, a square wooden stool to stand on so everyone could hear me.

The sun was low in the west, and a dazzling array of colors glowed in the evening sky—purple, pink, gold. "I have come to tell you about the One who put those colors in the sky," I said. "He made the sun, the mountains, the trees and everything else you see." I began to tell them about Jesus Christ and how He desired to save them from hell and give them eternal life. As I told them that Jesus had died to forgive their sins, and that God had raised Him from the dead, the Holy Spirit fell on the crowd.

Some got down on their knees under the Spirit's conviction, wailing over the sins they had committed. Others laughed uncontrollably as the joy of the Lord overtook them. The evening became a celebration of dancing, singing and shouting before the Lord. A new church had been born, in fulfillment of these words from the book of Acts: "And the Lord added to the church daily those who were being saved" (Acts 2:47, NKJV).

I have often been asked why so many miracles occur in Africa while they seem to be so rare in America and Europe. I believe it is because the African people have a simple faith, and that pleases God. When they hear His Word, they believe it, and then God blesses them.

In the West many people think they are too smart and too sophisticated to simply believe and accept God's Word. Instead, they question everything, including the Bible, and that displeases God. When simple people accept and believe what the Bible says without question, God blesses them. If we do not accept the Gospel the way a little child accepts what his parents tell him, then we miss much of God, because He reveals His mysteries to the simple-hearted. As Jesus said in Matthew 11:25–26, "I praise you, Father, Lord of heaven and earth, because you have hidden these things from the wise and learned, and revealed them to little children. Yes, Father, for this is what you were pleased to do."

When we accept His Word simply, without criticizing and doubting, God blesses us and we are able to see even more of His truths. I am not saying that we should stop going to school, learning or getting degrees. God created the universe and everything in it, and I believe that He is pleased when His people pursue knowledge and wisdom. But we must not get so caught up in that pursuit that we forget the simple truths of God.

6

Fishing for Souls

I stayed on a few days to teach the people what I knew about the Bible, which did not take very long. Nor did I know very much about structuring this new church. I knew that every church had a pastor and that Sunday was a special day because it was on this day that Jesus rose from the dead. I did not yet own a Bible, so we did not have the New Testament to guide us.

We did, however, have the Holy Spirit to instruct us, and He did. In more than 25 years since then, as I have traveled and spoken in churches all over the world, I have been amazed at how closely those first churches I planted in Africa followed the pattern set forth in the New Testament. As soon as I felt confident that the fledgling church was going to spread its wings and fly, I headed back out on the road.

Over the next few months I spent many nights sleeping out in the open and others on the dirt floors of huts crowded with young children. My one pair of sandals flopped up and down on my feet when I walked. I had walked at least a thousand miles in those things, and they showed it—I might as well have been barefoot. God had taken care of me every step of the way; I always had food to eat and a place to sleep, even if my "bedroom" was not always comfortable. Even so, I needed a respite.

So when I reached the village of Tengani on the banks of the Shire River in southern Malawi, I decided to buy some fresh fish to sell at the local market. The fishermen commonly fish all night and return in the morning to sell what they have caught. I went to the river very early in the morning, before the sun was up, to meet the first fishermen returning with their catch. There were not many buyers at that early hour, so I was able to get a very good price.

I bought so many fish, in fact, that I had to ask the fisherman to help me carry them back to the compound where I was staying. Next I had to build a fire to cook them, so I borrowed an ax from my neighbor and went out into the bush to cut some firewood. As I was chopping wood, I heard a noise that I could not quite identify. Some creature was stirring in the bushes nearby, so I went to get a closer look. I hoped it was something I could kill, cook and sell along with the fish.

I stopped and waited. The noise sounded like it was coming from behind this bush. I slowly spread the branches . . . and came face-to-face with a huge python, coiled and ready to attack!

If I did not act fast, I would be caught in the snake's death grip, and there would be no escape. I actually stepped on the animal with my right foot as it waved its tail around trying to catch me. I thank God that in those days I was shorter than I am now; that huge tail swung just over my head. When it flashed by, I could hear the whoosh of the wind it created.

In terror I whirled around and raced for home as fast as I could. For two weeks, I was in such fear that I did not sleep well.

Though my days as a fish seller had not begun on a hopeful note, things improved quickly. For one thing, I met a young man named Bire, who was also a strong Christian, and he and I decided to work together. We traveled throughout the Thyolo District, selling fish in a dozen or more small villages and telling our customers about Jesus.

We carefully arranged the cooked fish so that it looked as tempting as possible, and I began calling out to people passing by: "Fish here! It's a beautiful day. Come and get some tasty fish. How about you, sir? If you want to have a wonderful time, you need to have some of this fish!" I was so filled with joy because of my faith in Jesus that I could not help but joke and laugh and have a good time with the people who came to us.

"Are you a follower of Jesus Christ?" I asked a tall, thin woman who wore the traditional brightly colored *chitenje* skirt and an equally colorful scarf wrapped around her head.

She shook her head and took a step back. "No . . . I am not."

"That's a shame. I would give you the fish for half price if you were. Do you know anything about Jesus?"

An older, heavyset woman stepped forward. "I'm a believer!"

"You are? Praise God! Half price for you."

"Who is Jesus?" someone else asked.

"Jesus Christ is God's only Son," I explained. "He came into the world to forgive our sins, so we can live with God in heaven forever." I started out talking to one person, but a crowd quickly gathered, drawn by the Holy Spirit. By the time I had finished my talk, a dozen or more people were kneeling to receive Jesus Christ as Lord and Savior. Bire and I gave all of them a huge discount. We were not making much money, but we did not care.

This went on everywhere we went; in every village we started a church. We cared more about sharing the Good News than we cared about selling fish, but the more we shared the Gospel, the more fish we sold.

More Miracles

We also witnessed frequent healings. In one village a woman whose back was bent and stooped came to buy fish from us. She shuffled along as she walked, her head tilted so far forward that she seemed to be bowing continuously. As soon as I saw her, I felt the Spirit say, *I want to heal that woman.*

I asked her how long she had been that way. "Since I was a girl," she replied. "Almost as long as I can remember."

"Jesus Christ, the Son of God, wants to set you free," I told her. Then I laid hands on her and prayed that God would be glorified through her healing. I knew she was going to be healed because God had already told me so; I was merely the means through which He was going to show His power.

Excited gasps swept through the crowd as her bones and joints began to pop and crack. She grew taller, and straighter . . . and finally stood completely erect. The gathering exploded into applause, and people from throughout the market area came running to see what the excitement was all about. Many souls were won for the Kingdom that day!

Other times I would jump up on our stand and shout, "Come on, everyone, this is where you can find fish and freedom. Come get fish! Come get freedom! I guarantee you, this fish is going to make you happy!" People came to see what we were so excited about, and we were eager to tell them.

Because we were friendly and happy, we had the approval of the people. They knew they could trust us; our price was fair and our scales were honest. They also liked the fact that we were respectful. We were polite young men who did not drink, take drugs or leer at the attractive women.

No matter where we went, ours was always one of the busiest stalls in the market, and some of our many competitors hated us for it. They made rude comments to us and threatened to beat us. But the more they threatened us, the more

God prospered us. I would not be at all surprised to learn that they tried to harm us, but if they did, God protected us.

As we continued to make our rounds from village to village, we found that all of the churches we had planted were growing in numbers and spiritual strength. People we had led to Christ often told us how much they loved us and brought us food. We always got a great response from the people, and we had wonderful favor given to us by God.

Life was good in Tengani, and Bire and I had a wonderful two years of selling fish and telling people about Jesus. But there were so many lost souls who needed to know the love of Christ, in Malawi and across southern Africa.

God was calling me on.

7

Back from the Dead

Everywhere I went people wanted to hear about Jesus; some had heard the Gospel before, but they had it all mixed up with tribal religion and spiritualism. Some people told me they were followers of Jesus but then refused to take off the talismans they wore to protect themselves from evil spirits.

Within six months I had preached in perhaps thirty villages, starting a church in each. As I entered a community I would sometimes go to the market, find a group of men sitting under a tree and ask if I could join them. Then I would tell them about Jesus. Other times, I looked around until I found the biggest or fanciest house in a community. I figured it must belong to the chief or mayor of the village, so I would knock on the door and explain that I had an important message for the people. It always helped to have the leader on my side, and, of course, the fact that I went to the chief to ask his help showed that I respected his authority, which did not hurt my cause.

In one village, the chief banged a gong to let people know that an important meeting was taking place. People streamed in from their fields, their homes, everywhere. The chief told them, "This young man has something very important to say. I want you to listen to him because he speaks the truth."

It was amazing that I got such respect, although it was not me but the Holy Spirit. I was still just a boy and I was not an eloquent speaker—more proof that God will use anyone who is yielded to Him.

"Raise This Child, Lord!"

In one village where I held a crusade fifty or sixty people came to hear me preach on Monday night. On Tuesday fewer than half that number showed up. I felt a bit discouraged because crowds usually became larger, not smaller.

Then on Wednesday morning the village chief came to see me. "You will have to stop the crusade," he said. "Come back some other time."

"Why?" I asked. "What's wrong?" He explained that a little girl had died in the village the previous day and the entire community was in mourning. This was why the attendance had fallen off so sharply the night before.

"I am so sorry to hear that," I told him. "Would it be all right if I came to see the family to offer my condolences?"

"I think that would be fine."

I followed him to one of the larger houses in the village. Inside, six women sat weeping and clinging to one another for comfort, including the dead girl's mother. The child's body lay on a mat on the floor, wrapped in strips of cloth in preparation for burial. The chief introduced me to the child's mother and then hurried out to attend to other business.

"I am very sorry about your little girl," I said. The mother nodded and began sobbing. Wailing went up from the other women in the room. "Would it be okay if I prayed for you?" I asked. The women nodded, and so I began to pray.

Now, the book of Genesis says that when God created Eve from Adam's rib, "God caused the man to fall into a deep sleep; and while he was sleeping, he took one of the man's ribs and then closed up the place with flesh" (Genesis 2:21). Later, the Bible tells us that Abraham "fell into a deep sleep" when God was getting ready to make His lasting covenant with the patriarch (see Genesis 15:12).

This is what happened to these women when I began to pray. They all seemed to fall into a deep, trancelike sleep. As I kept pressing in, praying in tongues, unsure of what God would do, I looked in the Bible for a word from the Lord. I turned to Micah 3:7, "So the seers shall be ashamed, and the diviners abashed; indeed they shall all cover their lips; for there is no answer from God" (NKJV). This was not at all encouraging. While the ladies carried on their sleeping, I kept praying in tongues; finally I walked toward the girl and started unwrapping the burial cloths. When I had uncovered one of her hands, I put my fingers into the hand. Suddenly she grabbed my finger, startling me. When I began to recover from my shock, she said, "I am hungry."

I did not have any food, but when I looked around I saw a half-empty bottle of Coca-Cola. I picked it up and put it to the child's lips; she gulped down the remaining liquid. I helped her up from the mat and took her to her mother, who was still asleep. I gently touched the mother's arm. "Mama, your daughter is back." The woman's eyes opened—just a crack, but wide enough for her to see her girl standing there.

Immediately she jumped out of that chair and began screaming at the top of her lungs.

Then everyone was shouting and crying all at once. A couple of the women were so frightened that they ran out into the village screaming hysterically, thinking they had seen a ghost. Others were jumping up and down, hugging each other and shouting for joy. People came running from throughout the village to see what the commotion was all about.

Word spread rapidly that God had restored this precious child to her mother. I went straight to the village chief and asked him if he would give me permission to resume my crusade; of course he said yes. Everyone came to the crusade that evening to hear about the amazing love of Jesus Christ.

Reaching Out to Mozambique

At about this time I began to hear whispers of terrible things happening in Mozambique, and my heart began to yearn for my home country.

My homeland was embroiled in a brutal civil war, and thousands of refugees had streamed across the Zambezi River into Malawi. Most of them had left everything behind: houses, fields, belongings. They came with only the clothes they wore and terrible tales of atrocities. They told of armed men storming into peaceful villages, killing men, women and children with automatic weapons. Innocent babies were slaughtered; livestock had been stolen and fields set ablaze. I even heard reports of people being burned alive and that many children as young as ten or eleven years old were being forced to serve as soldiers.

This civil war began in the late 1970s with attacks against troops loyal to Mozambique's socialist government, Frelimo. These attacks were carried out by a rebel group known as Renamo. If it sounds confusing, it was. The Frelimo government was not popular in Mozambique because of its Marxist policies, but many remained loyal to it because they remembered that Frelimo had led the fight for independence from Portugal. Renamo guerrillas were also guilty of vicious attacks on civilians.

The war, which lasted until 1992, left nearly one million people dead and drove another five million from their homes. It was a horrible time for the people of Mozambique; so many fled their homes that one out of every ten people in Malawi was a refugee from Mozambique.

For the most part the civilian population of Mozambique did not know or care what the fighting was all about; they were innocent victims caught in the middle. Many were already desperately poor, and now they had a bloody war to contend with—misery piled on top of misery.

The more I heard about the goings-on back home, the more I felt the stirring of God to preach to my fellow countrymen. I had heard that thousands of refugees were living in a camp in Towe, in the district of Nsanje in southern Malawi. These were my countrymen and they needed to know the love of Jesus; I set my sights on the refugee camp.

When I arrived I found that the needs of the people were overwhelming, despite the efforts of some relief organizations that were doing what they could to help. There was no way they could have been prepared for the many thousands who streamed across the border; poverty and filth were everywhere. There was not enough food, not enough water, not enough medicine, not enough shelter.

And, certainly, not enough Jesus.

I saw young mothers with sunken eyes trying desperately to nurse their children, but they themselves were so malnourished they could not produce milk. Children who should have been running and playing sat listlessly in the dirt, too hungry or sick to do anything but stare off into space. It broke my heart to see them suffering like that, and I wanted to reassure them that God could and would meet their needs, if only they would turn to Him and put their trust in Him.

I did my best to share His promises, such as "Weeping may stay for the night, but rejoicing comes in the morning" (Psalm 30:5) and "Come to me, all you who are weary and burdened, and I will give you rest" (Matthew 11:28). I shared the divine assurance in Isaiah 61:3:

> Bestow on them a crown of beauty instead of ashes, the oil of joy instead of mourning, and a garment of praise instead of a spirit of despair. They will be called oaks of righteousness, a planting of the LORD for the display of his splendor.

I spent three months in that camp, preaching God's love and compassion to those who had seen so much of man's hatred and indifference to suffering. Hundreds came to hear God's Word, and once again He confirmed it with signs and wonders, including healings. I was especially grateful that God used me and the other believers in the camp to bring many young people to Him.

Some of the refugees were openly hostile to the Gospel when I first tried to talk to them. One young man glared at me when I asked him if he wanted to come to our service. "Why would I want to do that?" he asked sarcastically.

"We have music." I smiled. "It's fun; and I'll tell you all about God. You know He loves you."

He did not crack a smile. "You can keep your God," he said. "I don't want anything to do with Him."

"But He loves you so much that He—"

"They killed my father," he interrupted.

"Oh, I'm sorry." I reached out to touch his arm, but he pulled away.

"You can keep your love, too." He spat out the words as he turned on his heels and walked away. "All I can think about is how it's going to be when I make them pay for what they did!"

He was not the only one in that camp living for revenge. There were hundreds of them, and if we failed to reach them with God's love, the cycle of hatred and killing would go on and on and on.

Our small band of believers met together every day. As we sang and celebrated God's goodness, people throughout the camp were drawn to us, including many teenagers. We had so much joy in God's presence, they naturally wanted to be a part of it.

Every so often I would see that angry young man, and when I did I always said hello and told him, "God loves you." He always turned away. But as time went by, he did not turn away quite as fast or seem nearly as angry. Then one wonderful day, I gave an altar call and watched him slowly make his way to the front of our tent, where he fell on his knees and surrendered his heart to Jesus.

Let me tell you something: Never give up. God can soften the hardest heart. If you have been praying for a loved one for twenty years, do not stop! God will save people from sin; He will deliver them from bondage to drugs or alcohol. His love can melt a heart of stone—so, again, never give up!

Homeward Bound

After three months in the refugee camp, the church I had started there was large enough—and by the grace of God strong enough—that we could hand it over to a full-time pastor. Many of the people asked me to stay on, but I said no for two important reasons.

First of all, I did not know the Bible as well as I wanted to. I had bought my first Bible while in Tengani, and I had been devouring it. Some things were difficult to understand, however. I had even discovered that some of the "Bible stories" I had talked about in my sermons were not even in the Book. The people deserved to have an educated man as their pastor—someone who could teach them exactly what God said on every subject, not an uneducated eighteen-year-old like me; I needed to go to Bible school.

The second reason I said no was because I knew God was calling me home to Mozambique. I needed to be on the front lines, ministering God's love to those in danger and serving as a peacemaker in my homeland.

Over coffee one day I told one of my church leaders about my intention to return to Mozambique. He was shocked. "But you can't . . . you don't . . ." he sputtered, his face grave.

"I'm leaving in two weeks," I told him.

"You'll be killed!" he shouted.

I shook my head. "God will protect me."

"Listen, Surprise, it is far too dangerous there," he protested, reaching over and putting his hand on my knee. "I've been there. I've seen it."

"I have to go," I said. "It's what God wants me to do."

Neither one of us knew what else to say, so we were silent for a moment. At last my friend gave a loud sigh and leaned back in his chair. "I hope you know what you're doing. But please, spend some more time in prayer about this."

I nodded. "I will."

"Mozambique is full of people with guns, and none of them have the slightest regard for human life," he said. "Are you willing to be a martyr?"

"I am," I said.

8

Land Mine

He was not alone in advising me against going back to Mozambique. Even on my last Sunday, when I stood up to say good-bye, our new pastor urged me not to go. "Surprise, why don't you wait until the war is over?" he asked. "You can serve God right here."

Other voices from the congregation joined in. "Don't go!" "Stay here!" "We need you!" And so on. It was flattering, of course, but I knew they were not seeing things through God's perspective. I recalled a passage I had just read in the book of Acts, in which the apostle Paul's friends had tried to stop him from going to Jerusalem:

After we had been there a number of days, a prophet named Agabus came down from Judea. Coming over to us, he took Paul's belt, tied his own hands and feet with it and said, "The Holy Spirit says, 'In this way the Jewish leaders in Jerusalem will bind the owner of this belt and will hand him over to the Gentiles.'"

When we heard this, we and the people there pleaded with Paul not to go up to Jerusalem. Then Paul answered, "Why are you weeping and breaking my heart? I am ready not only to be bound, but also to die in Jerusalem for the name of the

Lord Jesus." When he would not be dissuaded, we gave up and said, "The Lord's will be done."

Acts 21:10–14

I had to be like Paul; no matter what anyone said, I had to go where God sent me.

My destination was Tete, a city with a population of around 100,000, on the Zambezi River. To get there I took a bus to the town of Mwanza, and then I walked to the border outpost of Zobwe. Renamo soldiers came to Zobwe twice a week to escort convoys through the war zone. No one could go into Mozambique without a military escort.

Zobwe had once been a peaceful little border outpost. Now the place was full of soldiers with automatic weapons slung across their shoulders. There were hundreds of them. Everywhere I looked, I saw soldiers with guns.

Otherwise Zobwe did not look like much. The town sat in the middle of gently rolling hills of red clay, surrounded by mango trees and sugar cane fields. There were some thatched huts and a few businesses—mostly fueling stations that catered to big trucks. In the center of the village stood a huge concrete building that in "normal" times served as the regional police headquarters. Now it also served as a base for an international peacekeeping team made up of soldiers from Zimbabwe, Malawi, Mozambique and other countries in the region.

Zobwe was also full of people trying to get into the war zone: drivers with trucks full of cargo, Roman Catholic nuns, businessmen, doctors, nurses, students—people from nearly every walk of life, anxious to reach the eye of a dangerous and growing hurricane of war.

Watch Your Step

An old man asked me where I was going and why. When I told him I was on my way to Tete, he shook his head. "You can get killed over there." He nodded in the direction of the border.

"I've heard," I replied. "Guns, guns and more guns."

"Guns?" he snorted. "That's not the worst of it. I'm talking about land mines."

"Land mines?"

"Thousands of them. One false step, and . . ." His voice trailed off.

That night I sat before the Lord as the sun sank in the west. As is often true in Africa, the sunset was dazzling in its beauty, splashing the sky with color. I felt the pure joy of God's presence and fell on my knees in awe.

It was an amazing feeling to think that I had a personal relationship with the One who had created the sun and bathed the world in light. People had warned me not to go into Mozambique. I knew I was facing terrible danger, yet there I was with a huge smile on my face, feeling as if I did not have a care in the world.

Thank You, Lord, I prayed. *Thank You for this beautiful world You created. Thank You for loving me. Thank You for your grace and mercy. My life is in Your hands.*

The world seemed so peaceful. It was impossible to believe that people were shooting and killing each other just a few miles away.

That night dozens of us slept on the veranda of the police station; there were so many of us crowded onto that porch that you barely had room to roll over. I managed somehow to get a few hours of sleep, although I slept lightly because I doubted that everyone could fit into the trucks in the convoy. Some people were going to be left behind, and I did not want to be one of them. As I "slept" I clutched a canvas bag that held all my possessions. The bag contained one very nice pair of shoes, a few clothes, a packet of chewing gum, some shaving lotion, a razor, a few other odds and ends and my money.

At 5:00 A.M., I was awakened by sounds of whistling and singing. "What . . . ?" Who was making all that noise at this hour? I sat up and looked around, not awake enough to remember where I was. My mind went back to the night the voice had told me to leave my home and family. Then it all began to come into focus.

The soldiers had arrived to take us into Mozambique. The sound I heard was the whistling and singing of the troops as they marched into the staging area; waiting there was a convoy of about twenty buses and trucks of all types, military and commercial.

There was no way I could get onto the first bus, so I hurried to the second. I was met by the driver standing in the doorway with his arms folded across his chest. "Full," he said.

I pushed my way through the crowd toward the third bus, but the door closed just as I got there. It, too, was full. That was when I felt the first drops of rain splatter on the top of my head.

What was I going to do?

Lord, I prayed silently, *I thank You that You are in control. Take me through this so that I can serve You and do Your will.*

People were scrambling into the assortment of trucks, including several flatbeds that were better suited to a cargo of bananas and oranges than human beings. In fact, some of them were loaded with fruits and vegetables for Tete. People had to shove aside the produce to find a place to sit down. At least those trucks had rails to keep you from falling out.

Here was one that looked like it might have room for one or two more. "Can I get on?" I asked the driver.

"That it?" he asked, eyeing my bag.

"Yes." I nodded, holding up the bag so he could get a better look.

He jerked his head in the direction of his truck. "Get on."

I climbed up and onto the bed of the truck. I do not know for certain how many other people were on that vehicle, but I would say at least 15 or 20 men and women had managed to squeeze in among the bananas, oranges, mangoes and other fruit headed to the market in Tete. A heavyset middle-aged man in a dashiki scooted over to make room for me. "Thank you," I replied as a few more raindrops fell.

"We're going to get wet." He smiled, looking up at the threatening sky. He was right. We would probably be soaked to the skin by the time we covered that distance on Mozambique's dangerous, pockmarked highways.

"The Lord is in control," I said. "Perhaps the rain will keep us safe."

My new friend opened his mouth to reply, but before he could get anything out, we were interrupted by the driver. "Here," he said as he handed us a large piece of plastic sheeting. "For the rain."

The engine of the huge military truck carrying mine-detecting equipment roared to life, followed quickly by the engines of all the other vehicles in our convoy. Our driver hurried to the cab, climbed in and turned on the ignition.

Twenty sets of headlights cut a path of light through the darkness. The sun had risen above the horizon in the east, but the day was still dark and gloomy. Our truck lurched forward as we unrolled the plastic sheeting to cover ourselves from the rain, which had become a steady drizzle. Over the next hour we must have put that tarpaulin up and then taken it back down at least half a dozen times. It was hot under the plastic, so we would get out from underneath it. But the weather was still cold and wet, so we would get back underneath it.

Our truck was somewhere in the middle of the convoy, which was led by the minesweeper and then three or four trucks full of soldiers in camouflage carrying automatic weapons. The soldiers whistled and sang as we rolled along, their voices echoing across the muddy red-clay landscape. I cannot remember the exact words of the song they sang, but the gist of it was "Everything is fine. You are safe because the enemy is defeated, and no one will dare come against us today."

At last, the sun broke through the clouds, the sky began to clear and the tarp was put away for good. Nobody said much as we bounced along; we were lost in our thoughts. We would not have been able to hear each other anyway; the noise was deafening as the vehicle bounced up and down, up and down, in and out of one pothole after another. My hands shook, my teeth chattered and my head ached.

Besides bouncing up and down, we also drifted from side to side as our driver tried to avoid the potholes. But there were literally hundreds of them, and there was no way he could miss them all.

BAM! Someone gasped as we slammed into a particularly deep hole. I had to admit, that was scary!

Held by the Arms of God

Ahead of us, the minesweeper whistled as it checked for explosives. It was not the most pleasant sound, but it was comforting just the same, because it meant we were safe as long as we did not stray from the path.

Before we could relax from our dive into the last pothole, our driver swerved to the right, apparently to avoid another huge pothole. When he did, we drifted a few meters off the road.

That was too far.

KA-BOOM!

My ears rang with the sound of the explosion. I felt myself somersaulting through the air. Flames licked at my feet, and thick, black, choking smoke enveloped me.

Land mine! I was going to die. There was no way any of us would survive.

Then, suddenly, I saw a powerful pair of arms wrap themselves around me, sheltering me from the explosion. I was suspended in air, looking down on the burning, twisted wreck that had been our truck. God had spared my life and was protecting me.

From my vantage point, I could see that the truck itself had been lifted into the air by the force of the explosion and had crashed down into the bush. The area where it fell was littered with charred bodies—and body parts.

Those huge, protecting arms gently put me down in the middle of the road. I looked up and saw a truck skidding right toward me. The driver had stomped on his brakes, but everything had happened so fast. Had I survived the explosion only to die beneath the wheels of this huge lorry?

I sat in the road, unable to move, not from any injury but because I was in shock over what had just happened. Dirt and gravel flew out from behind the huge tires. The vehicle shuddered to a stop within five feet of me.

For the second time in minutes, my life had been spared.

Before I could get out of the way, soldiers with their weapons drawn came running. "Get down!" they shouted. They began pulling people out of the trucks. "Get out and get down!"

Boom! Boom! Boom! They fired into the bush and waited for an enemy response. When no one fired back, they told us we could get up. Evidently it had not been an ambush. We had just strayed too far off the road and hit one of the millions of land mines that had been planted in Mozambique. (Even today there are more land mines in Mozambique than any other country in the world, and they are still killing and maiming innocent civilians.)

The commander of the convoy wanted to know how I had come to be in the middle of the road. "I was on the truck," I mumbled.

"That's impossible," a sergeant scoffed. "Everyone who was on that truck is dead."

"Not me," I said.

"You were not on that truck," he insisted. He changed his mind when two of his soldiers helped me get to my feet and he saw that the legs of my trousers had been singed by the fire. Also, a strong odor of smoke and burning metal clung to me. That noxious smell would stay in my nostrils for weeks.

The commander ordered a medic to examine me. The doctor felt my arms and legs, listened to my heart and lungs and had me turn my head in various directions.

He shook his head and put his stethoscope back in his bag. "He's fine."

"Fine?" the commander demanded. "How can he be fine?"

The medic shrugged. "I don't know. He's had some hair burned off his arm. But as far as I can tell, that's about it."

Tragically, everyone else had been killed; in fact, they had all been burned beyond recognition. I was dazed and in shock, overwhelmed by the sheer evil of what had just happened. The image of those burned bodies and that mangled truck is etched into my brain forever, although it would be only my first glimpse of the horrors men are capable of doing to each other because of the sin nature.

The army had been prepared for this. Teams were dispatched immediately with body bags to pick up the corpses, which were piled onto one of the remaining trucks. Then we prepared to resume our journey.

Still in a daze, I did not know where to go or what to do, so some young men about my age helped me climb into the back of a van, into which many of the dead bodies had been dumped. I felt that I was in a dream, half in this world and half in the next.

Suddenly the door of the van slid open and an army officer stuck his head inside. "This truck is overloaded," he said gruffly. "Some of you have to get off. There's room in the next vehicle."

All of the men got out of the van. We headed back toward a big blue box truck with a Zimbabwe license plate and climbed into the trailer. A few minutes later the siren sounded for the convoy to begin rolling.

I sat down against the wall, closed my eyes and hoped I could go to sleep. I was just starting to drift off . . .

KA-BOOM!

The thunderous explosion echoed through the countryside.

For a moment I thought I was having a nightmare. Then I heard voices shouting, people running, and I knew. The convoy had hit another mine. We all jumped out of our vehicle to see if there was anything we could do to help.

It was too late—of course. My mouth dropped in astonishment when I saw what had happened.

The van I had been ordered out of had been destroyed. The force of the explosion had ripped that van completely in half. Everyone inside had been thrown out, their bodies scattered for hundreds of feet in all directions. Among the dead were a tiny girl, just barely old enough to walk, and a little boy of perhaps four. They had barely begun to live, and now they were gone.

I knew that God had spared my life, not because I was any better than those who had died, but because He had a job for me to do and He meant for me to complete it. I was to preach the Gospel and save men, women and children from eternal damnation in hell. God did not want any of the people in the van to die; far from it. But His strongest desire is that no souls should be lost forever in hell.

For the second time in fifteen minutes, soldiers were dispatched to do their gruesome business of placing charred remains into body bags. Once again, most of the corpses were stacked up like firewood, and we headed on our way. I say *most* because this time some of the bodies were left in the bush. It was even more dangerous to be traveling after dark, so our commander was anxious to get us to Tete before sundown.

As a result some of the remains were left for the hyenas and vultures.

Voices in My Head

We made it the rest of the way to Tete without another disaster. But I was tormented by Satan the whole time.

The voices of people who had warned me not to go to Mozambique echoed through my head. They were so loud and insistent that I could not even think of anything else. "Surprise, you'll be killed!" "It's dangerous—you're taking your life into your hands." "They don't care who they murder." "You have no idea what you're getting yourself into." Over and over, the voices called my name, mocking me. I clapped my hands over my ears, but nothing could shut out the noise.

I was not the only one who was suffering. All around me, people were sick because of the horrors they had witnessed and for fear that it could happen to them as well. Some vomited on the floor; others had diarrhea or wet themselves. They could not help it—shock had taken away their ability to control their bodily functions—but the stench was overwhelming. The dreadfulness of the next few hours is beyond my ability to describe.

Just an hour before sunset we finally rolled into Moatize, a town on the outskirts of Tete. I was relieved to see the streets full of government soldiers. The convoy rolled to a stop just outside a football stadium. Soldiers marched up and down the remaining eighteen vehicles in our convoy and announced that we could use the bathrooms in the stadium to get cleaned up.

I am sure that our appearance was repulsive. Many wore clothes that were caked with vomit. Others reeked of urine, or worse. In "normal" circumstances, we all would have been ashamed and embarrassed. We were neither: We were just glad to be alive.

As I slowly made my way into the stadium, it suddenly occurred to me that I did not have my bag. What had I done with it? I ran back to my truck.

Nothing. It was gone. All my money, all my clothes, everything I owned in the world. Gone.

9

Fire in the Night

To all outward appearances, I had hit bottom. I had no money and nowhere to go. But it was only in losing everything I had that I discovered the peace that comes from relying totally on the mercy and grace of God. I had nothing, but I had everything because Christ was in charge.

I spent the next several weeks living in a camp for internally displaced people in Moatize. Thousands of families were living in tents here, most of whom had lost their homes to the war. Many had also lost family members and friends to the conflict. They desperately needed to know the love of Jesus.

God had brought me here safely to share the Gospel with these shell-shocked people who had suffered so much. When I first arrived in Moatize, the negative voices in my head were still yelling at me, telling me that I had made a terrible mistake in coming back to Mozambique and that I was going to pay for it with my life. But when my mind cleared, I saw perfectly well what God had done to protect me and bring me here. I had made a radical decision in returning to Mozambique, and the Lord had confirmed my decision and opened the way before me through perilous circumstances, as He did for the Israelites through the Red Sea. I now knew that I could not obtain what

God had for me unless I was willing to pursue it in a radical way. Since that day I have been determined not to let anything prevent me from doing what God has called me to do.

It was not for my sake that God protected me in such a miraculous way; it was for the sake of people in Mozambique who were on their way to hell because they did not know Jesus!

I began going from tent to tent asking people if I could have a few minutes to tell them about Jesus. Within a few days we had a small group of new believers, and I preached the Gospel with all my heart because I knew God was with me and would help me. During much of that time I never knew where my next meal was coming from, but God always provided. One day I was preaching outside the camp when an old man with white hair and a toothless mouth came up to me, leading a young goat. He bowed in my direction and gestured for me to take the goat.

"No, no," I protested. "I can't take your goat." The man was obviously in need, and the goat was a precious gift; in the United States or western Europe, it would be like someone giving you a brand-new car. There was no telling how long the man had to work to get that goat.

"You must take it," he insisted. Once again, I tried to turn him down. "It is a gift from God," he said.

What else could I do? I took the goat back to my tent, slaughtered it and ate well for several days. Sometimes I wonder if that "old man" was really a man at all.

For six months I traveled from village to village in Tete, telling people about Jesus and sharing my testimony in local churches, and many came to the Lord. Some of those trips into the countryside were dangerous; more than once I heard the sound of automatic gunfire in the distance as Renamo rebels and Frelimo troops engaged each other in battle.

While I was in Tete, God instantly gave me the language of Nhungue. I saw many salvations and healings, in even greater numbers than when I was in Malawi; miracles took place every day. My faith grew to a higher level. There was such an acceptance of what I was saying—everyone was believing and coming to Christ. The word of God spread throughout the cities of Tete, Matundo and Moatize, and the people were encouraged.

Even today, the same power that was in Jesus—that raised Him from the dead—is in us. It is in you; if you open your heart and receive it, it will manifest in you. The Lord can use you in greater ways, and His desire is that all would be willing.

Back to School

After a while I was ready to move on. It was time to pursue my education, which meant going to school in Beira on the coast of Mozambique. I asked the Lord and He provided an airplane ticket from a Christian brother. This was my first experience of flying, and despite all the divine protection I had personally witnessed, I was frightened. Before I got onto the plane I knelt down in the airport terminal to pray, confess my sins and give thanks to God.

Some of the people who passed by laughed at me, and I realize now that they must have thought I was crazy. Once I was on the plane, I started praying again. I was so fervent that the flight attendant asked me to pray more quietly. Forty-five minutes later I was safely on the ground in Beira, stepping into the next part of my destiny.

Beira is Mozambique's second-largest city with a population of nearly half a million. In Beira I obtained my secondary school diploma and then went on to nursing school. Amazingly, even though I had been out of school for years, I finished first in my class and discovered an aptitude and love for mathematics.

Of course, school always took second place to my main interest, which was telling the lost about the salvation available through faith in Christ. But I managed to obtain a degree in nursing, afterward moving to the nearby city of Dondo, where I took a job working in a local hospital. Mozambique was desperately in need of doctors and nurses because of the war, and I tended to many severe injuries during those days.

As time went on, three young men joined with me in the work of evangelism. We walked miles together, preaching the Gospel and praying for the sick. We were bound together not only by our love for the Lord but because we also had a love for singing. We called ourselves the New Jerusalem Singers and began singing at churches throughout central Mozambique.

Samito was quite a bit taller than the rest of us, and every day he wore a bright yellow shirt with a red leaf pattern on it. I could always see him coming from a very long way off!

Faria was very thin and painfully shy, but he was determined to chase miracles all the time. His was a rich, deep faith, and although there was a sense of frustration in him if we did not see a miracle as we prayed for all the children in the Dondo School for the Blind, his faith never wavered. His determination to run after the next miracle ignited all of our faiths.

The other member of our team was Eliya, who was just a boy, barely into his teens and perhaps not even that old. He always went along with whatever the rest of us wanted. He was light skinned and talkative, the sort of fellow who keeps things humming along at a high pitch; he also had a great attitude. "You are adults, so I will follow you and do whatever you tell me to do," he said, and then he backed up his words with actions.

I was the oldest of the four, and though I was not really much older than they were, I felt like all three of them were my sons. They were orphaned like I was, having lost their parents in the war. I shared everything I had with them, and through my part-time job at the hospital I made sure their needs were met.

When we were not singing or preaching, we spent much of our time fasting and praying. There were so many hurting people in Mozambique—blind, lame, deaf—and we longed to show them that God's power could make them whole in body and spirit. For me the most important thing was learning to step out in faith, to be willing to take bold steps and trust God for everything. I was building up my faith like a weight lifter working his way up to heavier weights. I was also learning the importance of seeking God's will at all times, rather than running ahead of Him into areas where He had not commanded me to go.

We had a friend named Chico who often sang with us. Chico was a little guy with a big attitude. He had an opinion on everything, often taking the opposing point of view just because he loved a good argument. Not that Chico was a hothead; one of the most amazing things about him was that he always seemed cool and calm, even while he was driving up your blood pressure with his contentious remarks!

Another amazing thing about him was the music he played on his homemade three-string guitar. That boy loved music, and whenever I saw him I knew that little guitar was not very far away.

Sadly, Chico was not a follower of Christ. I talked to him many times about his need to accept Christ as Lord and Savior, but he always put it off.

One bright, sunny afternoon, we decided to go by and talk to him about the Lord one more time. So we headed for the village of Mafarinha on the eastern outskirts of Dondo. We wound our way through the thatched-roof homes, under the many mango trees that were full of fruit and past the wells of the village until we reached Chico's home. Chico's parents had died when he was just a boy, and he had built himself a simple hut next to the house of his brother and sister-in-law.

As always, Chico was happy to see us, and, as always, he had his guitar with him. He was sitting in front of his house, strumming, and he called out a greeting when he saw us coming up the path. "Hello! Have you come for some music?"

"No." I smiled. "We've come to tell you about new life in Jesus Christ."

"Yes," he said, pointing to the Bible I was carrying. "I see you have brought your book."

"Chico," I said, putting a friendly arm on his shoulder, "when are you going to give your life to Jesus?"

"We can talk about that later," he said. "First, we sing!"

That is what we did; we sang for an hour or more. Then we spent some time reading the Bible and talking about what God was doing in our lives. After that we went back to singing. We kept singing praises to God as the shadows grew longer and darker, as the sun sank below the horizon and as darkness covered the land.

By the time we finished, it was late and we were all feeling tired and sleepy. Because it was a long walk back to the city, we decided to spend the night in Chico's hut. There was not much room in there for the five of us, but two of us lay on one side of the central pole that supported the roof, and three lay on the other side. I quickly fell into a deep sleep.

Although I had spent most of the day singing praises to God, I had a terrible dream: A dark, murderous phantom was after me and my friends. The fiend's head was perhaps two meters high, and it had enormous long teeth and eyes that were ablaze with fire. I tried to run but my legs would not work. The monster was coming closer, closer, closer. It was so close now that I could feel its hot breath on my face. I was about to be devoured, and there was nothing I could do. I tried to call out the name of Jesus, but when I opened my mouth, nothing came out.

I awoke with a dramatic start. For a moment I still thought the phantom was there, flames shooting out of the monster's eyes and nostrils. Suddenly, to my horror, I realized that the flames were real—Chico's hut was on fire.

Scrambling up, I shouted to the others, "Wake up! Wake up! Fire!"

Outside I heard the unmistakable rat-a-tat of machine gun fire; then a thunderous explosion rolled through the night. An artillery shell had landed nearby.

The fire blocked the hut's front door. There was no other way out—there was no other door and no windows. We ran to the back of the structure to get away from the flames.

The heat was suddenly intense; burning thatch from the roof fell all around us. We knew we were probably going to die, either by being burned alive in the fire or ripped apart by fifty-caliber machine gun bullets.

We began digging frantically at the mud walls, trying to punch out a hole so we could escape. The machine gun fire continued outside, punctuated by occasional blasts from bazookas or small-arms fire. There were screams, shouts—people were dying all around us.

"Come on," I shouted. "It's now or never!"

Together we gave one final kick to that wall, and it crumbled, spilling us outside into the darkness, just as the last of the ceiling caved in.

10

Massacre

We had beaten death!—but only for the moment. The air was thick with blinding smoke that stung our eyes and nostrils, and the sharp odor of gunpowder was overwhelming. We gasped for air, coughing up the smoke that filled our lungs.

Someone yelled, "Catch them! Catch them!" I took off running, although I could not see where I was going. "Please, Lord," I said, "help me!"

"Shoot them! Shoot them!" Shots rang out and I tensed my muscles, waiting for the bullets to find their mark. Praise God they missed me!

I kept running, silently praying for Chico and my other friends. I had no idea what had happened to them or if they were alive. The sky glowed red and explosions sounded all around me as I ran past one burning hut after another. I felt as if the world had come to an end.

I do not know how far I ran—a mile or two perhaps, maybe more, away from the carnage and into the bush. When I saw headlights, I skidded to a stop and ducked behind the nearest tree.

A whistling sound filled my ears, and something whooshed

over my head. The headlights belonged to a government truck with a rocket launcher mounted on the back; government forces were firing rockets at the Renamo rebels. Chico's little village had been caught in the crossfire and was taking a pounding from both sides.

Somehow I managed to get safely past the Frelimo forces, making it all the way to our pastor's house in Dondo. When I got there, I pounded frantically on his door. "Pastor Noah! Pastor Noah!" I could not shake the feeling that the Renamo killers were still pursuing me.

A light came on inside. "It's Surprise!" I shouted.

"Surprise? Just a moment." The door flew open, and in the lamplight I saw anxiety on Pastor Noah's face. He was a gentle, kindly man who cared deeply about people—a man full of the Spirit and power of God. "What is it, Surprise? Are you all right?"

"May I come in?"

"Of course."

"Renamo," I said. "They burned all the houses."

"Where? When?" He got up, went to the door and looked out. "Where are your friends?"

"I don't know if they survived."

Pastor Noah wanted to go out and look for them immediately, but I knew that was much too dangerous; we had to wait for daylight. We sat and drank coffee while I reported everything I knew about the rebel attack, which was not very much.

A couple of hours later, as night gave way to another bright, sunny day, Pastor Noah and I went back to Chico's neighborhood, hoping to find some news of our friends.

I wish I had never gone. What I saw that day still haunts me.

Government troops had collected all the dead and lined them along the railroad tracks, like so many bananas, for families to identify and take away for burial. The line of burned, bloodied corpses stretched for hundreds of yards: mothers and their children, grandfathers and grandmothers, teenagers, entire families. Some with eyes open, faces contorted by fear and agony. Others so badly burned they were barely recognizable as human beings.

Anguished wailing rose up from survivors as they discovered their family members and loved ones among the dead. Hundreds of people made their way along the tracks, praying they would not find the bodies of those they loved.

Devastation stretched out in all directions; smoke still drifted up from heaps of rubble and ash where thatched huts once stood. Houses made of concrete or bricks had also been destroyed, and walls that still stood were pockmarked with craters left by large-caliber bullets.

For me this was a new revelation of man's capacity for evil. How could human beings do this to other human beings? What made it even worse was that this destruction had not come at the hands of an invading army; the people of Mozambique—*my* people—were doing this to each other. Even worse than that was that most of those who had died, perhaps all of them, were innocent civilians who did not even know what the fighting was all about.

Alive

"Surprise!"

I spun around and looked into Chico's familiar face. "You're alive!" I shouted as we embraced each other.

"I'm so glad to see you," he replied, his voice cracking with emotion.

"Is your family . . . ?"

"My brother and his wife are fine," he nodded.

"Thank the Lord!"

"Yes. But her parents are dead. And all of her family." I did not know what to say. After a moment of grave silence, we turned our attention back to the corpses, hoping that we would not find our friends among them.

"They set the houses on fire, and then they shot people when they tried to escape," Chico said, his voice quivering with anger and grief. "If we had been able to make it out of the door, we would all be dead." He paused, swallowing. "Some people chose to stay in their houses and burn to death."

Nearby a woman screamed and fainted as she discovered the body of someone she loved. I did not know if it was a husband, a child or some other relative, and I prayed that God would take her in His arms and comfort her.

By God's grace none of our friends were among the dead, although Eliya's extended family had been swept away in the carnage. Eliya himself was in the hands of the local police, who had taken him into protective custody after they found him wandering aimlessly, obviously in shock. Samito and Faria had found each other in the mayhem and were looking for the rest of us. By God's grace we had all survived.

I have been asked if my faith ever wavered in the midst of such horrible circumstances. The answer is no. God did not plan this, and He did not will it to happen. It came as the result of man's disobedience and selfishness. During the worst of times I knew that God's heart was broken. I felt His grief. He would have given anything to bring peace—and, in fact, He did: He gave His only Son.

But despite the circumstances I always had joy in my heart. I knew that God was in control and that as horrible as the situation might seem at the moment, He could and would bring something beautiful out of it. Satan may seem to win a battle every now and then, but ultimately the victory belongs to God and His people!

I also knew that something good would come out of the horror. As always happens when disaster strikes, many people turned to God—including our guitar-playing friend, Chico, who became a powerful preacher and a full-time pastor, as well as a police officer.

11

A Hunger for Knowledge

Because I had witnessed such a massacre and so much evil, my relationship with Jesus changed after that night. Before, Jesus had been the most important thing in my life—by far. Now having lived through this horrendous event I felt that nothing else mattered; I felt that anything that earthly life offered was only an illusion that could evaporate in a moment and that anything I did that was not done for God was a waste of time.

I therefore decided to leave my career in nursing and devote myself to full-time ministry. By the grace of God I had always enjoyed great favor as a preacher of the Gospel, even though I was barely out of my teens. When I went into villages to preach, the people could have dismissed me because of my youth. Instead they treated me with respect and listened with interest to what I had to say. Even in the churches I attended, men and women who were much older and who had been following Christ for much longer than I had gave me honor and respect. Still, I was lacking in my knowledge and understanding of God's Word, and I hungered to know more. I wanted to go to Bible school.

One night, as I was waiting before God, I suddenly felt that He wanted me to go to South Africa. *South Africa, Lord?* I asked. I had never been there and was not particularly anxious to go. I had heard about apartheid, and I knew that black people were often mistreated in South Africa.

Johannesburg, I felt Him say. That was all.

Over the next few days I prayed often for further instructions, but none came. Meanwhile the feeling that I was supposed to go to Johannesburg grew stronger. I did not know anyone there; I did not know where I was to go when I got there. But I knew I was supposed to go, and I figured that God would take care of the rest. It seemed He wanted me to trust Him one step at a time, and I had learned that He is completely trustworthy.

So, trusting Him, I bought my tickets. I had enough money for an airplane ticket to Maputo and a train ticket from there to Johannesburg. I said good-bye to my friends and set out on a new chapter of my life.

It was early morning on January 3, 1990, when the train pulled into Johannesburg. My mouth fell open when I saw the sun glinting off the tall buildings. I had been in some fairly large cities before, but I had never seen anything like this. After the train rolled to a stop, I sat rooted to my chair for a few minutes, taking in the grandeur of this huge city of glass and steel. Finally it occurred to me that I was the only one still on board, so I snatched up the small bag I had brought, which contained all of my worldly possessions, and headed down the stairs to . . . only God knew where.

From the train station I wandered down the street until I came to an intersection. Left or right? I decided to turn right. I walked down crowded sidewalks, past shops and restaurants full of customers. Shop windows displayed an amazing array of expensive merchandise. Late-model cars rolled past as I silently prayed that God would show me where He wanted me to go.

I came to another intersection and paused, trying to decide which way to go. While I was standing there, a man came up and asked me in perfect Portuguese if I needed directions. Once again God had gone ahead of me, as He did that day when I first stumbled out of the jungle and was met by Mr. Lukas: He provided me with Jim Teckleyberg.

Jim was a strong Christian who owned a farm in the area. He took me home to introduce me to his wife and children. He also made arrangements for me to travel to Durban for an admissions interview at the Bible school there, Kwasizabantu Mission, and he generously financed my education.

At the time of the interview, I did not know the school was limited to English-speaking students; as I could not speak English, I would be automatically excluded. In my ignorance I went for the interview anyway with the director of admissions, Pastor Fun Sabise.

Pastor Sabise stood up to welcome me as I was ushered into his office. "Sit down, Mr. . . . ."

"Sithole," I said. "Surprise Sithole."

"Surprise?" he said. "That's an unusual name."

I laughed and explained how I came to be named Surprise. He asked me about my family, my background, my education and my reason for wanting to attend Bible college. We had a pleasant conversation that lasted for perhaps fifteen minutes. I thought it went very well.

At the end of our time together, he said, "You speak English very well. Where did you learn it?" I did not know what to say; all this time I thought we were speaking Portuguese! All I could do was laugh. God had given me the language when I needed it. What an amazing God! He supplies all our needs!

As for school itself, I loved learning God's Word. For me there was nothing difficult about studying the Bible, and I did very well. What a wonderful time I had during those years—drinking in the wisdom of men and women who had been walking with God for many years. In Bible school the

Lord also gave me the Zulu language, and I went on several outreaches as a translator, even though I had not had any formal training in English or Zulu. I often went out with the others to preach in nearby towns and cities, and I was witness to many wonderful acts of God.

After my years in Bible school I thought briefly about joining the ministry staff of a church. There were many relatively affluent churches in South Africa, and I would have been much better off financially if I had taken this route. But my heart was with those people in the remote villages who would never have a chance to hear about Jesus unless someone like me told them about Him. Therefore I went back to doing what I had done first in Malawi and then in Mozambique—going from farm to farm and village to village to preach the Gospel and plant churches.

I walked long distances every day. Usually I had no place to sleep, so I spent the night out in the fields, under bushes or anywhere else I could find to lie down. I often took comfort in Jesus' words, "Foxes have dens and birds have nests, but the Son of Man has no place to lay his head" (Matthew 8:20).

I did not mind sleeping out in the open. What I did sometimes find difficult was the lack of food. Most of the time I survived on discarded morsels of food. Sometimes I had to scrape off the ants before taking a bite. I would brush them off, telling them, "Okay, this is my food now. You go find something else." The ants that did not listen to me would become an extra bit of protein. I admit to having eaten some stale, disgusting-looking scraps in an attempt to fill my aching stomach, but God always blessed me and they tasted good once they were in my mouth.

Sometimes I found fruit and vegetables that had fallen on the road, such as sugar cane, pawpaws and tomatoes. There were a few other delicacies that crossed my palate from time to time, such as the lion meat I was given one day after farmers shot a beast that had ventured too close to their village. Even with the Lord's provision, walking such long distances every day took its toll. I was weak and dehydrated from lack of water, to the point that I suffered from frequent nosebleeds. Still, I was doing God's work, and that made me happy, even though people sometimes made fun of me because I was so poor.

Encounter with Demons

It was during my travels through South Africa that I had my first encounter with demons. I met a Mozambican named Shouva who, like me, had been born into a family of witch doctors but had come to know Jesus Christ as his Lord and Savior. When I met him he had been a Christian only about a week. He was a very calm, gentle fellow, and I liked him immediately.

One day as we were praying together he suddenly started foaming at the mouth, as if he had just eaten a bar of soap. Before I could ask him what was wrong, he fell down and began rolling around on the ground, tearing at the grass and shouting, "Take off your friend! Take off your friend!" I did not know what it meant, but I did not like the sound of it.

When he finally got up, he stood there staring at me through wild, bloodshot eyes. He was shaking visibly, and I was certain he was about to attack me. *He must be crazy*, I thought; I would be in danger if I did not get away. I considered fleeing; we had climbed to the top of a small mountain to spend some time alone with the Lord, so it would do me no good to shout for help.

Then God brought something to my mind: Shouva had told me that when his mother had died, he had kept the thatch basket she used as a witch doctor as a keepsake. He must have unwittingly invited demonic influences into his life, and they were now manifesting through him.

So instead of running, I stretched out my hand in his direction. "In the name of Jesus, out!" I shouted. He staggered backward. I said it again. "In the name of Jesus, get out!" Although I had not touched him, he fell over backward, crashing to the ground with a thud. Then he stretched his arms out—and seemed to go to sleep. I stood staring down at him, wondering if he was going to jump up suddenly and attack me. Instead he slept peacefully for a few minutes; then he opened his eyes, cleared his throat and sat up.

"What happened?" he asked. He had no memory of his strange behavior. I told him God loved him very much and that I would stay and pray with him as long as he wanted me to. Shouva went on to become a strong leader in the church in South Africa.

Annalie and Gart

Not long after this, as I was coming out of a school where I had been preaching, I was surprised to see a middle-aged white couple walking toward me. The woman was a warm-looking, buxom lady, and the man with her, who I assumed was her husband, was thin, very tall and bearded. The woman gave me a friendly hug, and her husband did the same.

I was astonished.

"My name is Annalie," she said.

"And I'm Gart," the man smiled. "Gart Nell."

"Surprise Sithole," I said.

"We're pleased to meet you, Surprise," Annalie said.

I tried not to show how surprised I was by their friendliness. This was South Africa in the early 1990s, when apartheid was still the law of the land. In these years the country was moving toward healing, but there was a great deal of violence in South Africa committed by those both for and against apartheid. It was not always safe for white people to be in black areas of the country and vice versa. It was unusual to see a white couple in a black township, and for them to approach and embrace a black man was downright startling.

"We heard you talking about Jesus," Annalie said. "You're a believer, then?"

"Yes, I'm an evangelist," I explained.

Annalie touched her husband's arm. "Us too," she said.

"That's right." Her husband nodded.

"Do you live around here?" Annalie asked. Excitement showed on her face. Her eyes were filled with gentleness, and her presence had a calming influence on me. I could tell right away that both of these dear people were filled with the Spirit of God.

"I don't really live anywhere," I said. "I just travel from town to town, telling people about Jesus."

"But where do you stay?" she persisted.

I shrugged. "In the bush."

"You sleep out in the open?" Annalie asked.

"Yes, that's right."

She looked down at the ground, and I thought she was going to cry—especially when she saw the ragged, worn-out shoes I wore. She did not know it, but the shoes were not really that old. Christian friends had given me many new pairs of shoes over the years, but walking ten to fifteen miles over rugged terrain every day wears them out quickly.

She and Gart exchanged a meaningful look, and he nodded. "Why don't you come home with us?" she asked. "We don't have a lot of space, but you can share a room with my son."

"But, but . . ." I spluttered, not sure how to respond. "You don't really know me, and . . ."

"And?" She smiled.

". . . and I'm black."

"We can see that," Gart laughed. "We can also see that you're a servant of the Lord, and we'd be honored to have you stay with us."

I protested because I was afraid that having me in their home would get them into trouble—but they would not change their minds. And of course having a soft, warm bed to sleep in sounded awfully good to me.

"Do you have any . . . uh . . . clothes, or . . . ?" Annalie asked.

"Only what I'm wearing," I answered. "And my Bible."

"Well, come on then," Gart said. "We'll take you home."

I climbed into the back seat of their Jeep, and we headed off toward their house, which was not far. They lived in Malalane, a small town that sits right at the entrance to South Africa's famous Kruger National Park. Kruger is one of the world's largest national parks, spreading over seven thousand square miles of wilderness and serving as home for so many animal species, including buffalo, elephants, impalas, giraffes, leopards, lions, rhinoceroses, wildebeests and zebras.

I suppose their home was not all that big by Afrikaner standards, but it looked like a palace to me. How wonderful to have a roof that would keep the rain off, and walls that would protect me from the wind and animals that might be in the mood for a little midnight snack.

Their son, Rehgart, who was eleven at the time, was a delightful boy who seemed to have no problem at all sharing his room with me. "Great!" he said when his dad told him he had a new roommate. "Hey, Surprise, do you like cricket?"

"I don't know much about it," I admitted.

"I'll teach you," he said. "You'll love it!" Just like that, I felt at home, as if I had always been a member of the family.

That night, Annalie cooked a marvelous meal, while Gart brought in a bed frame and mattress they had in storage. I supposed this was not the first time they had had a guest in the house. How wonderful it was to lie in a bed that night, and to take a shower and feel fresh. It was so much better than waking up under a tree or a piece of plastic!

The two years I spent with Annalie and Gart was a very special season for me. The love Annalie gave me was the strongest I had ever experienced from another human being, and I loved her as if she were my own mother. She took great delight in comforting, encouraging and lifting other people up. Her life was marked by kindness and gentleness, and her ready smile warmed many hearts in addition to mine. Her favorite subject was grace, which she understood so deeply and showed by her example. Whatever we spoke about, the subject would always lead back to grace.

The Peace Is Shaken

When I was living with Annalie and Gart, I used their house as a base while I continued to preach in surrounding villages. Sometimes Annalie would come with me, driving me from place to place, which made everything so much easier and better. Together we traveled all over South Africa and even to Beira in Mozambique and Nairobi in Kenya, preaching the Gospel and telling everyone about the love of Jesus.

I was blissfully unaware that word was spreading through the neighborhood that the Nells had a black man in their house.

I did not spend much time there because I was usually out preaching. But one afternoon I happened to be home when Rehgart returned from school. He stormed into the house, slammed the door and threw his book bag on the floor. "I've had it!" he shouted angrily. "I'm not going to take it anymore!"

"Not going to take what anymore?" I asked, coming out of the bedroom.

His face turned red when he saw me. "Oh, Surprise, I didn't know you were home."

"What has you so upset?" I asked. "Do you need to talk about it?"

"No, it's okay," he shook his head. "It's really nothing."

"Are you sure? Can I pray with you?"

"Oh, Surprise," he said, fighting back tears, "some of the kids at school say such awful things about you!" He stomped over to the sofa, plunked himself down with a thud and folded his arms across his chest. "I'm sorry. I didn't want to tell you about it," he said.

I sat down beside him. "What do they say about me?" I asked.

"That they don't know how I can bear being in the same house with you," he said. "They say you're dirty, and that you probably stink."

"And what do you say?"

"I tell them that you don't stink, that you're the cleanest guy on earth. But they call me names . . ."

I got the impression that the teasing and bullying went on constantly. He tried to defend me, to fight back against his tormentors, but he was outnumbered. I put my hand on his shoulder. "I'm very sorry," I said.

"It's not your fault," he said. "They're just so . . . so stupid."

"They can't help it," I said. "It's the way they were raised. But maybe it *is* my fault. Perhaps I should leave."

"Leave?" He gave me an angry look. "No way! You're part of the family. You belong here."

Just a few days later, I was in the house reading my Bible in the evening when I heard loud voices in the backyard. I went outside to see what was going on.

A heavyset man with a round face stood on the other side of the fence, engaged in a shouting match with Annalie. Actually, that is not exactly right. The man shouted while Annalie tried, in her usual kind way, to get him to calm down.

He glared at Annalie, his face angry and red, as a stream of profanity flew out of his mouth. "Please," she said, "there's no reason to use such language."

"I'll use any language I please," he shot back. "You people are destroying this neighborhood, and we're not going to stand by and let it happen."

"We?" Annalie asked.

"All of us!" he shouted. Before he could explain further, he saw me watching from the doorway. "There he is now!" He pointed at me. "You tell him he's not welcome here."

Annalie put her hands on her hips. "I've tried to be reasonable with you, sir, but you are way out of line."

"Don't you tell me . . ."

"It's no business of yours who we have in our home. Good day."

He was not finished yet, but Annalie turned on her heels and stormed back into the house, adding to his anger by taking my arm and escorting me back inside. "You'd better tell him to watch his step!" he threatened.

"I said, 'Good day!'" Annalie returned, quietly shutting the door.

The man continued to yell at us, his insults and threats peppered with swearing. It bothered me much more that he took the Lord's name in vain.

Gart had been in the bedroom helping Rehgart with some homework, but now they both stood in the doorway wearing worried expressions. "What was that all about?" Gart asked.

"We need to pray," Annalie replied. The four of us got down on our knees and went before the Lord, while the angry neighbor continued to hurl insults and threats at us. We prayed for protection, courage and strength, and we thanked God for this opportunity to demonstrate His love. We also prayed for those who hated other people for nothing more than the color of their skin and asked the Lord to bless them and bring them into His Kingdom. We remembered this description of the scene in heaven from the book of Revelation:

After this I looked, and there before me was a great multitude that no one could count, from every nation, tribe, people and language, standing before the throne and before the Lamb. They were wearing white robes and were holding palm branches in their hands. And they cried out in a loud voice: "Salvation belongs to our God, who sits on the throne, and to the Lamb."

Revelation 7:9–10

By the time we finished praying, the angry man had apparently grown weary and gone back to wherever he had come from. Gart did not say much more about it that night, but I found out later that he had gone around the neighborhood and made it known that he was not going to allow anyone to threaten his wife or his houseguest. Gart was a kind, good-natured man, but he had a strength and ruggedness borne out of the difficult life of a missionary in the African bush. He was not the sort of fellow you wanted to mess with.

As for me, I was much more concerned for Annalie and Gart than I was for myself. They were like my parents, and it broke my heart to see what they were going through because of me. But they were unwavering in their support of me and did not want to hear any talk from me about leaving. I am sure I will never know all the ways they suffered because of their love for me.

On one occasion Annalie took me with her when she went to give her testimony in a church in the town of Komatipoort. When we got to the church door, one of the ushers blocked our entrance. "I'm sorry," he said, "but he'll have to wait outside."

Annalie smiled sweetly. "Pardon me?"

"Blacks aren't allowed in the church," he explained, nodding in my direction.

"Oh, but Surprise is my good friend," she said. "Surely you can make an exception for him."

I did not want to cause trouble, so I turned to go, but Annalie grabbed my elbow to stop me. What she was saying, really, was "If he can't come in, *I* won't come in." But she did it in such a charming way that it did not turn into a nasty confrontation. Eventually the church leadership relented, and I was able to attend the service, most likely becoming the first black man to ever see the inside of that church.

Love Letter

Every day the entire family arose at four o'clock in the morning and spent at least an hour in prayer. One morning, as we were praying near the computer, a sentence suddenly popped up on the screen:

I Want to Teach You My Faithfulness, My Kindness, My Love.

We were amazed. None of us had seen or written this sentence before, and there was no earthly reason why a message like this would suddenly appear on the screen. God Himself had written us a love letter.

Love was on my mind in those days. I was now in my late twenties and beginning to think about how good it would be to find a woman to share my life and my ministry. Every Tuesday a group of us met in Gart and Annalie's home to spend time fasting and praying for special requests. We wrote our requests on paper and put them on the table, and then each person would pick up one of those requests and take it before the Lord. One Tuesday I wrote, "Please ask God to bring me a wife."

Gart picked up my request, read it and then quickly flipped it into a nearby wastebasket. "Surprise doesn't have a request this morning," he teased.

"Yes I do," I said. "I want you to pray that God will send me a wife."

"I'll tell you what," Gart said. "I think you need to look for a woman named Tryphina. When you find her, you'll know that you've found your wife." He thought he was teasing, and so did I. We did not realize that God was speaking through him.

12

A Woman Named Tryphina

It was May 1995; I was still single and still wondering when God would send me a wife.

I sat in the back of a four-by-four double cab truck, squeezed between two pastors, as we rolled toward an evangelistic outreach in Zimbabwe—one of the countless trips I took to do ministry while I lived with the Nells. I was thrilled to be going along with several pastors and missionaries from Europe and North America, men of God I respected and loved deeply, to help translate their words into the Shona language. There was excitement in the air as we speculated about the salvations, healings and other miracles we were about to witness.

Suddenly the conversation around me began to fade away, and I seemed to be alone. In front of me I saw a large chalkboard divided in two; the top half was bright pink, and the bottom was sky blue. Oddly enough I had seen this chalkboard before—twice, in fact. But I had no idea what it meant.

As quickly as it had come the vision faded, and I was back in the truck, in the middle of a spirited conversation.

I closed my eyes and prayed silently. *Lord, You have shown me this vision three times, and I still don't know what it means. Please help me understand what You are telling me.*

I was brought back to the moment by a playful poke in the ribs from the pastor on my left. "Surprise, when are you going to get married?" he asked, a mischievous grin spreading across his face.

"That's right," said the man on my right. "You had better find a wife soon, because you're getting old!"

"Old?" I protested. "I'm only twenty-seven."

"Twenty-seven? Brother, you *are* old!" They could see that I was embarrassed, and they were not about to let up; all of them joined in the good-natured fun.

Suddenly it was clear to me that the vision I had seen was a message about my future wife. Someday, hopefully soon, I would meet the woman who would share my life, and when I did she would be wearing pink and blue. It did not mean that I would marry the first woman I met who happened to be wearing pink and blue. But it did mean that if I met a woman who was not wearing those colors, she definitely would not be the one God had chosen for me.

I said nothing to the men with me, but I felt excited. Could it be that I would meet "the one" in Zimbabwe? My mind was still focused on this happy thought as we passed the turnoff toward Bulawayo and drove toward Mutari.

All of a sudden, as we zipped along at about seventy miles per hour, I saw a man walking down the middle of the road just ahead of us—a tribesman with a bow and a quiver full of arrows slung over his back. We were headed right for him, but our driver made no attempt to avoid him. "Look out!" I shouted.

The driver stamped on the brakes and we squealed to a stop. By the time the car finally came to a rest on the shoulder of the road, we were sprawled all over each other, with Bibles and other materials flung everywhere.

After a moment the driver asked, "What? What happened?"

"You almost hit him!" I pointed at the tribesman, who was still walking down the middle of the road in the same direction we were heading.

"Him, who?" the driver asked.

The pastor on my left squinted out of the window and then shook his head. "I don't see anyone."

"He's right there!" I pointed again. "Don't you see him?" I could tell from the looks on their faces that they saw nothing.

The driver sighed and leaned back in his seat. "We could have been killed!"

"But you were about to run over that guy," I protested. He shook his head, restarted the engine and pulled back onto the highway.

The man was still there, walking in the same direction we were headed, but we did not get any closer than fifty meters or so. He continued walking ahead of us for some time, until he finally disappeared from view—yet another mystery for me to ponder.

The Sound of Footsteps

When we reached our destination, we found the villagers in terrible shape.

Many people were sick and hungry—some only days away from death by starvation. So many terribly thin children sat in front of their huts, too weak to run and play with other kids. Some had swollen stomachs and orange-tinged hair, both signs of severe malnutrition. Some mothers came to greet us, carrying children that looked like living, breathing skeletons, their skin stretched tight over their bones. Children's eyes are supposed to sparkle with hope; there was no sparkle in those eyes, nothing but despair.

The entire village was strangely quiet. There was no sound of children's laughter, no echo of women's voices as they gossiped at the local well, no babies crying. They were too weak to cry. If there had ever been a community that was desperately in need of the love of Jesus, it was this one.

117

As I made my way toward the circle of mud and thatch huts that made up most of the community, a young couple approached, carrying a small bundle wrapped in a tattered blanket. The woman reached out and placed the bundle in my outstretched arms. "Please pray," she pleaded. Her husband brushed a tear from his eye.

I unwrapped the blanket and found a little boy of about two years old. He was as light as a feather and burning with fever; I doubted that he could survive more than a few more days.

I closed my eyes and began to pray. As I did I heard the sound of footsteps behind me. Realizing that someone was coming to join me in prayer, I looked to see who it was—no one was there.

I closed my eyes and began to pray a second time. Again I heard the unmistakable sound of the ground crunching beneath someone's feet. I could also feel the presence of someone standing beside me.

I looked again—no one there.

When this happened a third time, I suddenly realized, *Oh—it's the man I saw walking down the middle of the road!* My heart was filled with joy because I knew the child would be healed. Sure enough his fever broke, his eyes opened and he smiled at me.

I knew beyond any doubt that God had heard my prayer and that the man I had seen on the road was one of His angels. He had been sent ahead of us to prepare the way for us. Many children were healed and their families saved before our time there was over.

After we had seen to the needs of the people in that first village, we went on to a second community, Chimayo, another two-hour drive away. By the grace of God the situation was better for the people who lived there. They had enjoyed better fortune with their crops, and their children were not suffering from malnutrition. Because they had enough to eat, they were not dealing with the diseases that prey on the weak and hungry.

My mind turned once again to the vision of the chalkboard, and I began expecting to meet a young lady dressed in pink and blue, but it did not happen. On the long drive back to our home in South Africa, my exhilaration over what I had seen God do was mixed with a bit of sadness and disappointment that I had not met the one God had prepared for me.

Could It Be?

I was also exhausted, so I decided to take a short trip to Beira, Mozambique, where I had tracked down a cousin named Anna. When I contacted Anna by telephone, she said she had plenty of room in her house and offered to have me come and stay for a few days.

Anna's husband worked in immigration, and they lived in a simple house made out of bamboo sticks filled in with mud and rocks. With its two bedrooms and sitting room that also served as a kitchen, and shaded by tall mango trees, it was a comfortable place for me to rest.

Early one afternoon, as I looked out her window, I saw a young woman passing by on her way home from school. Her arms were full of textbooks—and she was dressed completely in pink and blue!

I stood there for a moment, my heart beating rapidly in my chest. She was about to pass by; I had to do something fast.

I ran into the street and called after her. "Hello!"

"Hello," she responded, smiling shyly.

My heart was beating so fast I wondered if she could hear it. "I see your school books," I said.

"Yes?"

"Well . . . I need you to be my secretary. I want you to help me write the story of my life." I still do not know why I said that; it just came out.

She laughed and replied, "Okay, give me a pen and I'll write it."

"No, it's not like that," I said. I was so nervous, I hardly knew what I was saying—very strange for someone who had been face-to-face with death on so many occasions and who was very familiar with the power of God. "I need you to be my wife so we can spend our lives together."

I had not even asked her name, and I had already proposed. She threw back her head and laughed, but not in an unkind way. In addition to being beautiful she was gracious and kind; she could have told me to leave her alone or even run in the other direction, but instead she politely said, "No, thank you. But I would love to introduce you to one of my friends. She wants to get married, but not me—not yet."

That was not what I wanted to hear, but I said I would be happy to meet her friend; it was a way I could keep in touch with her. I told her I was staying with my cousin and invited her to come back the following day with her friend. She said she would.

It was only after she left that I realized I had failed to ask her name.

When I went back inside, I discovered that Anna had been watching my clumsy attempt to introduce myself. She took my arm and said, "It's okay, Vovo" (*Vovo* is the Portuguese word for *grandfather*, which my cousin had for some reason begun using as a nickname for me). "She's a very nice girl. But God will provide you with someone else to be your wife."

"But she is the one," I said. "I'm sure of it."

The next day she came back to see me as she had promised, but she came alone. Her friend, she explained, was busy. That made me very glad because I knew this girl was the one God wanted me to marry. We talked for some time, getting

120

to know each other, and I was delighted to discover that she was a believer who loved Jesus Christ.

This time I remembered to ask the important question I had forgotten previously. "You know," I told her, "I don't even know your name."

"Tryphina," she said. "My name is Tryphina."

13

White River

There is no way I can describe the joy that rose up in me when Tryphina told me her name. Before she left that day I again brought up the subject of marriage.

"I'm not ready to think about marriage," she said. "I have to finish school first."

"I'll wait!" I told her.

"What if you find someone you like better?"

"I won't."

She laughed again. "How do you know that?"

"I just know."

She got up, walked to the window and stared out for what seemed to me like a long, long time. Finally she turned around and sighed. "If you can wait until I finish school and you still feel that way, then we can talk about marriage."

That was the best I could hope for. She agreed that we could begin seeing each other so long as her grandparents, with whom she was living while she attended school in Beira, gave their permission. The next few days were among the happiest I had ever known, second only to the time I accepted Jesus Christ as my Lord and Savior. The more I got to know Tryphina, the more I knew that God had made us for each other.

All too quickly the time came for me to return to South Africa and continue the work God had called me to do. Before I left, Tryphina made a startling confession: About a month before she met me, she had begun fasting and asking the Lord to tell her about the man she would marry. As she left my cousin's house on the day we met, following my hasty proposal, she heard the Lord say, *This is your blessing.* That was the reason she decided not to bring her friend back to meet me the following day.

Before I left a friend of mine took some photos of Tryphina for me. I treasured those photographs and spent time gazing at them every day until I could see her again. Back in South Africa I often took out those photos and gazed at her face. We had only spent a few hours together, and yet I felt that my love for her was growing every day. God really had given me a supernatural love for this young woman.

When school let out for the holidays, I returned to Beira to see Tryphina. I had something else very important to do as well: I needed to ask her father for her hand in marriage. He lived in Angónia District in northern Tete Province, a two-day journey from Beira by bus. Fortunately for me Tryphina's grandmother liked me, so she agreed to go with the two of us on this very important trip.

This part of Mozambique had been hit hard by the civil war. Hundreds of thousands of people—about two thirds of the population of the district—had lost their homes to the fighting and fled to refugee camps in Malawi. Before the fighting, Angónia had been one of Mozambique's most productive farming regions, with fields full of maize, sorghum and other important food crops. Through God's grace, Tryphina's father had managed to hang on to his home and his land, but as our bus made its way into the mountainous district, it was clear that others had not had the same grace.

Indications of the war's destruction were still evident: Over there a rusted army tank sat in the middle of a field; here was an empty house, collapsing in on itself, with its walls pockmarked with bullet holes.

I was grateful that Renamo and Frelimo forces had signed a peace agreement three years earlier, which seemed to be holding. But I could not help wondering how many land mines were still out there, waiting for the unsuspecting traveler to wander in the wrong direction.

"No, no, *no*! I will not give you permission to marry my daughter!" Tryphina's father turned and glared at her. "I don't want this to happen! I sent you to Beira to go to school, not to look for a husband." Then he turned and stomped away.

This was certainly not the way I had envisioned things. I had expected Tryphina's father to see that I truly loved his daughter and to welcome me into the family; instead he was hostile from the moment we arrived. Tryphina's grandmother put her hand on my shoulder. "I'll talk to him," she said.

"I don't know if it will make a difference," Tryphina sighed. "He is so angry."

Her grandmother nodded. "I will see what I can do."

I did not sleep well that night. I lay in bed with my eyes wide open. I knew that God was going to work things out, but I was impatient; I wanted Him to act quickly.

And He did! I was amazed to learn the next morning that my future father-in-law had undergone a change of heart. When we met him for breakfast, he told me, without even a trace of a smile on his face, "Okay, I give you permission to marry my daughter. But you have to wait until she finishes school to get married."

"Yes, sir!" I exclaimed. "Thank you, sir!" This was, of course, exactly what we had planned to do in the first place, so it was fine with me. Later I discovered that Tryphina and her grandmother had reminded him that I had come all the way from South Africa to ask for his daughter's hand in marriage. This convinced him that I genuinely loved and respected her.

Walking on Air

As you can imagine, I was filled with joy when I returned to South Africa. God is so good! I never stopped smiling. But the enemy was not about to let up on me.

One time, when Gart and Annalie were gone for a month, I woke up in the morning with blurry vision. I sat up and tried to rub the sleep out of my eyes. "Ouch!" That hurt.

I threw back the covers, made my way into the bathroom and flipped on the light. In the mirror I could make out that both of my eyes had what looked like little pimples in them, and pus was oozing from them. Something was terribly wrong; I feared that I was losing my vision.

I spent that entire day fasting and praying, asking the Lord to heal my eyes, but when I went to bed for the night, my vision was still blurry and my eyes still hurt. Despite the pain I fell asleep quickly. At 2:00 a.m. a bright light in the room roused me. I was astonished to find that I was surrounded by people dressed in blue robes; three stood on my left and three on my right. It was as if I were lying on a table in an operating room and they were about to perform surgery on me. I did not feel frightened because the peace of God seemed to fill that room. My visitors said nothing, just continued with their work, and I eventually fell back to sleep.

About two hours later, I woke up again. The people in blue were gone, but my body was burning hot and I was drenched with perspiration. I got up, grabbed my Bible and went out into the darkness, hoping that the cool morning air would drive the fever away. I had a favorite place on the sandy riverbank nearby, where I lay down and began to pray. The cool air must have soothed my fever, for I drifted back to sleep. When I opened my eyes, daylight had come, and again I saw something hovering over me.

Snake!

I was practically face-to-face with what appeared to be a boomslang, a snake with venom so poisonous that a small amount can be fatal. It had descended from a nearby tree, and I was certain it was about to strike. Instinctively I jumped up and sprinted toward the river.

Wait! Something was moving in the water.

Crocodile!

I froze, waiting for the snake to strike my back. I figured it was better to die from a snakebite than to be devoured by a crocodile. If the snake killed me, at least people would find my body and know what happened to me; if the crocodile got me, I would disappear without a trace. I tensely waited for the fangs to sink into me, but nothing happened. I turned around to find that the snake had not come any closer. I had left my Bible sprawled open on the ground, and the reptile hovered over it as if it were reading God's Word.

I snatched my Bible out from under the creature and ran toward the house, hoping that the crocodile would not pursue me. I made it through the door, slammed it behind me and breathed a huge sigh of relief. Then I locked the dead bolt just to be sure I was safe.

Suddenly it occurred to me that I had seen that snake quite clearly. What was more, my eyes no longer hurt. I went into the bathroom, washed my face and examined my eyes in the mirror. The "pimples" were gone and my eyes were fine. I had been healed! I have since thought often about those "doctors" in blue. I assume they were angels, sent in response to my prayers.

A New River for Fishing

I stayed on in Malalane after Gart and Annalie moved to Durban, and I continued to preach throughout the area. Then one night I dreamed I was fishing, but I could not catch anything. In my dream I had been standing on the banks of a river for hours but had not had so much as a single bite.

I was just about to give up and go home when a woman walked up to me and said, "No, no! Throw your line into the white, clear water over there and you'll catch a lot of fish." She pointed toward a section of the river just downstream, where the water did seem to be especially clear and deep.

I did as she suggested and immediately felt the tug of a fish on my pole. When I pulled the line in to shore, I was astonished to see that I had three fish instead of one. "How is it possible to catch three fish at once?" I asked, delighted by my good fortune.

"I told you," the woman said.

I cast my line into the water a second time and quickly caught another fish. Then another, and another. The fish were so hungry they hardly waited for my bait to hit the water before grabbing it.

I woke up feeling both pleased and puzzled. God was trying to tell me something, but what? I did not have to wait too long to find out.

That very morning Annalie called from Durban to tell me that she had been praying for me, and the Lord had directed her to call and tell me that I was supposed to start a church in a place called White River. I had never even heard of White River, but what she told me was certainly in keeping with my dream. That night at church a man approached me and said he felt God was calling me to ministry in a new area. Then, after the service, I went forward for prayer and the pastor told me, "Maybe it will be painful, but I tell you, your post here is coming to an end."

Four times I had been told that it was time for me to move on, so that is what I did. In November 1995, I left Malalane and headed for White River, although I first had to get a map and find out where White River was! Although Tryphina was still attending school in Mozambique, I felt certain that White River was the place where we would build a life together.

I began searching for a roof over my head and was led to the home of John and Antoinette Robinson. They were wonderful Christians who owned several hundred acres, where they grew fruit and vegetables, including cabbages, onions and carrots, and they had many workers. They were remarkable in their generosity, opening up their farm and their hearts to me. They gave me the use of an old white concrete building, never questioning who I was or where I came from. This ended up being Tryphina's and my home for ten years, and we began to discover that this immense generosity was part of John and Antoinette's very nature. They trusted me and loved on me from the very start.

It was not long before I saw why the Lord had brought me here. Although the countryside was beautiful, many of the people were trapped in the worst sort of spiritual darkness. Alcoholism was rampant, and, as I was about to find out, demons were everywhere.

14

Into the Fire

*B*AM! *BAM! BAM!* What was that noise?

I sat up in bed and looked around. For a moment I was back on Chico's floor as Renamo mortar shells exploded outside. Then I remembered that I was back home in White River. My lovely bride, Tryphina, lay in bed beside me.

"Pastor Surprise!" someone shouted outside. "We need your help." Tryphina groaned softly and put a lovely hand on my shoulder. "What time is it?" she asked.

I squinted at the clock next to our bed. "Two thirty."

BAM! BAM! BAM! The pounding on our door grew louder and more frantic. "Please hurry!" shouted the man banging on our door.

Tryphina sighed, "We just got to bed an hour ago."

"I know." I threw back the covers and headed for the door. Tryphina quickly slipped out of bed, put on her robe and hurried after me.

"Pastor Surprise!"

"I'm coming!" I shouted, simultaneously unlocking and opening the front door. In the faint glow of the moonlight I recognized George, one of the men who worked on the farm. He had his arm wrapped around a young man of perhaps fourteen, who was shaking and trembling violently. "It's my son," George said.

"Yes, I see." I opened the door wider so they could come in. As they walked into the house, I reached out and touched Marcus on the arm. Before I could ask what the problem was, he pulled his arm away from me and screamed as if I had just touched him with a hot branding iron.

"I'll kill you!" he shrieked. He glared at Tryphina. "I'll kill all of you!" He began stomping around the room, alternately growling, shrieking and tearing at his own hair. "How long has he been like this?" I asked his father.

"He woke us up a couple of hours ago. He was screaming and trying to cut himself with a knife."

I had seen this before—many, many times.

Marcus had slumped onto the floor. His eyes stared off, as if he were looking into another world, and drool poured out of his mouth. "Marcus," I commanded, "look at me." He responded with a swear word and spit in my direction.

With the help of Tryphina and the boy's father, I managed to get my hands on his head. "In the name of Jesus Christ . . ." I began and bound the spirit afflicting him.

"Noooo!" Marcus shrieked. "Leave me alone!"

". . . come out of Marcus right now!"

"I won't do it! I won't go!" he wailed.

"Come out of him now, in the name of Jesus!" Marcus shivered and shook as if he were a volcano about to explode; and that is pretty much what he did, spewing vomit all over the floor—and me. Then he slumped over and was quiet. "Is he . . . ?" his father asked.

"He will be all right now," I assured him. "The demon is gone."

As usual, Tryphina had hurried into the kitchen to fetch the cleaning solutions and tools she used for the numerous occasions like this. If we worked quickly, we could probably be back in bed within another twenty minutes or so—perhaps we could even get another hour or two of sleep before the next person came seeking help.

I was often reminded of the villagers that came crying and seeking help from my parents, who really only wanted their money. My parents had always wanted me to follow in their footsteps, but instead I was being used by God to bring healing and hope in the name of Jesus. In a way I was making up for the harm my parents had brought through their involvement with evil spirits.

Life in White River

Tryphina had finished school in 1996, and we were married in December of that year. I was spending much of my time in Mozambique doing ministry, but I still considered White River to be my home. Although I was thrilled to have Tryphina as my wife, the wedding came at an intense emotional time for both of us. The week before we were to be married, my cousin Anna suddenly fell ill and died. It was a terrible shock, and we thought about postponing the wedding. But we had already waited what seemed like a lifetime, so we decided to go on with the ceremony, even though we were both numb with grief. It rained that day, which seemed fitting considering that we had both lost a lovely, precious friend.

I am embarrassed to say that we had no honeymoon. In fact, we spent our wedding night sleeping on the floor at the bus station in Beira. The following morning we boarded a bus that would take us home to White River—or at least get us started in the right direction. We spent the next three nights sleeping in bus stations. It was not exactly the honeymoon suite at a five-star hotel, but we really did not know what we were missing, and we were happy to be together.

When we finally arrived in White River, we moved into the white concrete house in the workers' compound. It was small to begin with, and our three rooms seemed even smaller when there were other people around, which there almost always were. Poor Tryphina really did not know what she was getting herself into! Those nights in the bus station were paradise compared to what awaited us in White River.

Looking back on it now, I wish we had had some time to go on walks, relax, talk about our future and just spend time learning to love each other. Instead we dove right into an intense period of ministry. We usually had four or five other people staying with us, and we had absolutely no privacy. There were always extra people at our dinner table—and with no sink or running water and a single hot plate in the kitchen, Tryphina worked wonders feeding the constant flow of people.

Like my father before me, I often brought home children and others who had nowhere else to go, although, unlike my father, I was motivated by the love of Jesus. (And unlike my mother, Tryphina always did her best to make these "strangers" feel welcomed and cared for.)

At the time I had no sense of what it must have been like for her. Sadly, I was too busy responding to the endless needs that came through our door to think much about anything else, including her or our marriage. A steady stream of people were always waiting to come into the house to be delivered, and when they were, they sometimes vomited, urinated or defecated—and sometimes all three—as the demons left them. It was up to poor Tryphina to clean up the messes.

I am embarrassed to think about how hard it must have been for her, but I have learned that it is not helpful to dwell on such things and let them linger in my heart, making me feel guilty. So now I laugh about it because it is in the past. When bad things happen to you, it is better to laugh so that you can forget them. If you do not laugh, you will not forget, and then you will continue feeling guilty. Laughter can be the broom that sweeps the junk from our minds. So we should laugh a lot to remove the unwanted memories and rubbish from our thoughts.

In White River it seemed that whenever anyone had a problem, others would say, "Go see Surprise!" Most of the people who came to us for help worked on the farm, so our days were much quieter than our nights. As soon as the day's work was over, right around five o'clock in the afternoon, the line would start forming at our door. Sometimes more than a hundred people would line up; some needed deliverance; others yearned to be set free from bondage to alcohol or other addictions. Many were sick or injured and could not afford to see a doctor. Tryphina and I made certain that every one of them had a chance to hear about the love of Jesus.

I am sure you are familiar with the story in the Gospels about the men who carried their paralyzed friend to Jesus for healing:

> Some men came, bringing to him a paralyzed man, carried by four of them. Since they could not get him to Jesus because of the crowd, they made an opening in the roof above Jesus by digging through it and then lowered the mat the man was lying on.
>
> Mark 2:3–4

That is a pretty good description of what it was like at our house, especially during the evening hours. I am not equating myself with Jesus, but because He allowed me to be the channel of His healing love, people flocked to our home, and we felt that we could not turn any of them away. Jesus, after all, healed the man who had been lowered through the roof.

This created a number of problems for us, including the fact that we did not have the plumbing necessary to take care of so many people. We had one outdoor toilet, which was, strangely enough, uphill from the house. Due to overuse, that toilet was often clogged and overflowing, issuing a foul-smelling brown stream that ran past our front door.

As you can see, we were not living in a subtropical paradise. Tryphina did not know the culture of our new home, which was entirely different in many ways from what she had always known in Mozambique, nor did she speak the Zulu language. We had no cell phone nor any outside communication. Even worse, she was often alone for days and weeks at a time while I preached the Gospel in the surrounding villages. In fact, during our first year of marriage, I spent only a handful of nights at home with my wife. The rest of the time, I was out doing what God had called me to do: the work of evangelism across the South African countryside.

I do not know what we would have done without the kindness of John and Antoinette Robinson. What dear, wonderful people! They first took me in on November 15, 1985, and they took care of me incredibly well. Every week I went to pray with them, and any time I needed anything I just visited them and they sorted it out for me. They treated me like family, and I even began interviewing all the applicants who came for work at their fruit and vegetable business. I was made to feel very much at home. They have become and remain to this day like my parents, and I love them dearly.

John and Antoinette always made it their business to ensure that we never went hungry, and they checked on Tryphina while I was away, ensuring that she was doing well and that her basic needs were met. Even so, because we were so poor and I spent so much time on the road, Tryphina took a job cooking and cleaning for a well-off family in the White River area. But after a couple of weeks of trying to communicate with her via gestures and pointing, her frustrated employers fired her.

I did my best to teach her the language, but she simply could not get it. Tryphina is a very smart woman, but the hours we spent together going over simple sentences only resulted in my frustration and her tears. When I failed to teach her Zulu, we tried Swazi. More frustration. English? A little better, but not much.

Then one day, after I had been out preaching in the bush for a couple of weeks, I came home and found her speaking English. I was so exhausted from my time in the field that I did not even realize it at first when she greeted me in a language she had never been able to speak before. After our hello kiss and embrace, it suddenly occurred to me that she had not been speaking Portuguese. "What did you just say?" I asked her.

"I said, 'I'm happy that you're home. I missed you,'" she replied.

"That's what I thought you said. When did that happen?"

"When did what happen?" She laughed.

I pulled her close. "You know what I mean . . . the English."

"I was just praying that God would help me, and then one day I was able to speak English."

Prayer! Why had I spent so much time trying to teach Tryphina how to speak English when I should have just prayed that God would give her the language supernaturally, as He had done for me?

Despite the difficulties of life in White River, it was a wonderful time of ministry. Our two oldest children, Enoch and Lovey, were born there, and God performed many miracles for our family—both great and small. When Enoch was just a baby, Tryphina and I once carried him into town. We had no money, no food, nothing. I do not even know for certain why we went into town.

As we were sitting on the steps of a building there, a pickup truck pulled to a stop in front of us, and two young white men got out. They walked up to us and, much to our surprise, held out a handful of money. "What is this for?" I asked.

"We just want you to have it," one of them said. "We can see that you are Christians, just from the way you are sitting." By the time we recovered from our shock, they had climbed back in their truck and drove away.

I still do not know how they could see our faith just from the way we were sitting. Perhaps they were angels. Angels or not, we were certainly thankful for their help.

Use What You Have

On another occasion I spent three days fasting and praying on the prayer mountain on the Robinsons' farm. At noon on the third day, the whole mountaintop was suddenly full of heavenly beings. I was waiting for a word from the Lord and believed that perhaps He had sent His angels to deliver His message to me. But though they were all around me, none of them spoke a word.

All of a sudden I fell into a deep sleep, during which I had a vision. The Lord Himself appeared to me and asked, *Why are you looking for another word? I gave you My word, I gave you faith and I gave you My Spirit. I have shared with you whatever I could give. So take courage, for I am with you. Use what you have.*

When I woke up, the heavenly beings were gone—but from that day forward, God began to increase His power in my ministry. When I came down from the mountain on Friday evening, I went to a service at the church. The angels that had appeared to me on the mountain showed up in the church that night, and we worshiped all night long. No one wanted to go home, and the service continued until midmorning the following day! One woman who was sick with AIDS was healed that night. The Bible says:

When Jesus had called the Twelve together, he gave them power and authority to drive out all demons and to cure diseases, and he sent them out to proclaim the kingdom of God and to heal the sick.

Luke 9:1–2

The Lord sends us to the world so that we can operate in the same way using these gifts that He gave us. We need to ask for and desire the gifts; as the Scriptures say, if we ask for bread, He will not give us a stone.

The Seven Churches of Sofala

After Enoch was born, I had a strong desire to reconnect with my family. Even though my cousin Anna had died unexpectedly, I still had some relatives living in Mozambique, and I wanted to tell them about my son.

In July 1997 I traveled to Beira for a two-week visit. During my short stay in Sofala Province, I planted seven churches. My first two converts were railway workers named Zachariah and Tom. After he surrendered his life to Jesus, Tom began holding regular meetings at his house. People came and accepted Christ, and then they, too, began churches in their homes. It is truly amazing to see how quickly the Word spreads when hearts are ready and hungry for God.

Later that year, in September and November, I made more trips from White River to Beira. Each time, I spent a week at one of the new churches, sharing and teaching the people God's Word. Then I sent them out to share what I had taught them with people in other communities. They always did as I asked with great exuberance and joy. Churches were being planted and nurtured by people who had been followers of Christ for only a few weeks! They did not have a lot of Bible knowledge or any degrees in theology, but they had passion for lost souls and a willingness to do whatever God told them to do, and the results were truly amazing. Years later I had an opportunity to visit many of those churches in Sofala Province, and I was delighted to discover they were still going strong and still faithful to Jesus.

15

A Woman Named Heidi

It was around the time I moved to White River that Heidi Baker came to speak at the church I attended. Rolland and Heidi Baker are missionaries who settled their ministry, Iris Ministries, in Mozambique in 1995 to be an outreach to the poor and orphaned in Africa.[1] As I listened to her talk about the work of Iris Ministries, I was very impressed. Her passion for God and her love for the African people were evident. As soon as the service was over, I made my way forward to tell her how much I enjoyed her talk. She had mentioned that Iris Ministries was headquartered in Mozambique, so we chatted briefly in Portuguese. I wished her well and told her that I would remember her and Iris Ministries in my prayers; then we said good-bye.

I assumed that this meeting would be the sum of my association with Iris Ministries, but a few weeks later Heidi showed up in a dream. I saw her standing on a small hill and calling to me, "Come over here. We need you!" A few nights later I had a similar dream. This time Heidi stood on the top of a tall building, again calling for me to come and help. Both dreams

1. For more information about Iris Ministries, see http://www.irismin.org.

were so vivid that I knew God was talking to me, and so I immediately made plans to travel to Chihango, a community about twenty miles from the Mozambican capital of Maputo. Rolland and Heidi ran a children's home in Chihango where they cared for more than three hundred boys and girls.

I arrived in the middle of a crisis.

The government of Mozambique had directed the children's home to be shut down after charging the Bakers with providing "unauthorized" food, clothing and other aid. They had been ordered to vacate the property in two days. It was an especially difficult time for several reasons, one of them being that Rolland was traveling in a remote area of South Africa and could not be reached.

The children loved Heidi, and she loved them back. Though she tried to shield them from the crisis they were facing, they knew something was wrong, and many were fearful and crying. They had already lost their parents, and they were afraid of being back out on their own again. I even heard a rumor that a reward had been offered to anyone who would kill Heidi.

Later that day I traveled to Boa Nova, where I was staying. A very strange thing happened to me in the night: Just as I drifted off to sleep, the phone rang, and when I went to answer it, I fell out of bed. I was sharing the room with a man named Matt, who had come from the United Kingdom to work with Iris Ministries. He called out, "Are you okay?"

"Yes," I answered. "I'm fine." The phone had stopped ringing, so I got back in bed and quickly fell asleep again.

Again, the phone rang and I fell out of bed when I went to answer it. Matt sat up when I hit the floor with a thud. "Brother, you fell out of bed again. Are you sure you're all right?"

"Yes, I'm fine."

I got back in bed and it happened a third time. "What is going on?" Matt asked. "Maybe you should sleep on the floor!"

"No," I said. "I'm just trying to answer the phone."

Matt laughed. "There aren't any phones here; there's no service!" Of course he was right. In my sleepy condition I had forgotten that no telephone service was available in Boa Nova.

Yet I had heard the phone so clearly. That is when it occurred to me that God was trying to get my attention—He was making it clear that He wanted me to do something I had not yet done: make a full-time commitment to Iris Ministries. I got down on my knees and silently told Him that I would do as He asked.

Their Ears Were Closed

The next day I joined a small group of people who met with some government officials to ask them to reconsider an order to stop teaching about God at the children's home. I hoped that the Mozambican authorities would listen to me because I had been born in Mozambique and spent the first fifteen years of my life there. I thought the fact that I was one of them—not an "outsider" from America or the United Kingdom—would give me a bit of influence.

But I was wrong. They resisted all reason, even though Rolland and Heidi had taken 320 naked, ragged, heartbroken children off the streets and had given them a chance for a decent life. Even better, these children had learned that they have a heavenly Father who loves and cares for them. But now, the authorities were going to undo everything. Like robots they kept repeating, "If they stop teaching about Jesus, they can stay. If not they have two days to vacate the premises." They were like those of whom the prophet Jeremiah wrote, "Their ears are closed so they cannot hear. The word of the LORD is offensive to them; they find no pleasure in it" (Jeremiah 6:10).

Of course the authorities knew that Iris Ministries could not agree to these demands. Everything Rolland and Heidi did for those children was borne out of their love for God and their desire to follow Jesus' command to feed, shelter and care for "the least of these." There was nothing we could do but withdraw to Iris Ministries' headquarters in Maputo and wait to see what the Lord was going to do.

We did not have to wait very long. As we gathered in prayer, we heard what sounded like music, far off in the distance. Was it our imagination? We stopped praying and listened. There it was again—the unmistakable sound of a favorite praise song of Rolland and Heidi's children. And it was getting louder, and stronger.

We all ran outside and turned in the direction of the music. "Look!" someone shouted. I could barely make out two small figures headed in our direction. We could not yet tell who they were, but they were singing as they came.

As they came closer, I could see two more behind the first two, and two more behind them—a company of little soldiers marching along, lifting praise to Jesus. "The children!" Heidi exclaimed, overwhelmed with joy.

She was right. The band of children marched toward us. These little ones—some as young as five or six years old—had walked the twenty miles from Chihango. We were overwhelmed by what these brave girls and boys had done, and by one very important question: How in the world were we going to feed and care for them? Nobody needed to worry. That was God's business, and He would take care of it.

Later several of the children shared the same story about what had happened. They had gone into the dining room for breakfast on the first day of the new "regime" and began singing praise songs at the top of their voices. A man blew a whistle and ordered them to stop singing, but they kept on. "Shut up!" he shouted. "I said, 'No singing.'"

The children continued to praise God.

"You will not be allowed to worship God here!" He blew the whistle again, and then he and several other members of the new staff began hitting the children with wooden paddles and their fists to get them to stop. That was when the children had walked out together. No one was going to tell them to stop worshiping the God they adored! They were also determined to find "Mama Aida" (Heidi) and "Papa Rolland," who had been so good to them.

Naturally the children were hungry and tired by the time they made it all the way to Maputo. A friend of the Bakers from the U.S. Embassy, Nelda Lawrence, came over with some chili and rice for the Baker family. She apologized that she did not have enough food for everyone, saying, "There's only enough for you and your two children."

Heidi shook her head. "They're all our children," she said, "and the Lord will provide." Then she ordered the children to sit down, prayed over the food and began dishing it out to them. Everyone ate until they were completely full.

Over the next few days, weeks and months, the miracles continued. Two other Christian organizations offered the use of some buildings to house the children. Someone donated a large piece of land, and someone else gave dozens of used army tents for the children to live in. God provided everything Iris Ministries needed to continue its work in an even bigger and better way than before.

I was astounded by the faith of those children. They were little boys and girls, powerless in the eyes of the world, but they were mighty warriors in the kingdom of God. Some prayed for hours every night and received supernatural visions and words of wisdom from the Holy Spirit. Their faith was strong, pure and unwavering, and I was constantly being reminded of Jesus' words: "Truly I tell you, unless you change and become like little children, you will never enter the kingdom of heaven" (Matthew 18:3).

Cholera!

Over the next several months, I was constantly traveling between South Africa and Mozambique. I had an immediate rapport with Heidi. We had a natural flow between us that the Lord used to bring many souls into His kingdom. I knew from the start that Heidi was a strong woman who would never back away from danger, but I will never forget the courage she showed when we went into a community that was in the grip of cholera.

Cholera is a terrible, highly contagious disease that causes diarrhea, vomiting and severe abdominal cramping. Without immediate treatment, death from dehydration often follows. Cholera also strikes quickly, growing from infection to full-blown illness within a day or two. The World Health Organization estimates that the disease kills as many as 120,000 people every year, warning that cholera can kill within hours if left untreated. This type of disease can be devastating to a small African village, where the nearest health care facility may be a day's walk away.

Most people would run in the opposite direction if they heard that a community had been ravaged by cholera. Not Heidi. She ran right into the fire.

I had just returned from a mission trip out of the area when Heidi gave me the news that cholera had broken out in our district. We headed immediately to the community that was at the epicenter of the outbreak. A long, white hospital tent had been set up in the middle of the town. Three doctors in green surgical scrubs stopped us as we tried to enter and escorted us back outside. "You can't go in there," one of them said.

We explained that we had come to pray for the children and ensure that their spiritual needs were being met as well as their physical needs. "I'm sorry," the doctor said, folding his arms across his chest. "You'd be putting yourselves at risk." His colleagues mumbled their agreement.

Heidi did not miss a beat. She kept insisting that God had sent us there to share His love with the children, and we would not leave until we had done so. We went back and forth like that for a while, but it did not take long before the doctors saw that we were not going to give up and reluctantly agreed to let us inside. When we did, the stench filled my nostrils and almost overpowered me. I stopped to catch my breath, but Heidi did not hesitate for a moment.

As my eyes adjusted to the dim light, I saw row after row of cots—hundreds of them, each cradling a person suffering from cholera. Beside each bed sat a cast-iron pot. Nurses were doing their best to keep the pots emptied, but they were fighting a losing battle.

Heidi walked straight into this disgusting, foul-smelling, life-threatening mess. She knelt down beside people to pray for them. She lovingly wiped the perspiration from their foreheads. She took children into her arms and hugged and kissed them—pouring out her life again and again. Her courage and grace amazed me, and I tried my best to follow her example.

Another miracle occurred at this time. These sick people were desperately in need of clean, safe water, and Heidi and I decided that I should go to the local market and buy all the bottled water I could find. The only problem with this plan was that once we were inside the quarantined area, there was no way we could leave until the medical authorities had determined that the threat had passed. Armed guards were stationed around the hospital tent to ensure that no one left the area. It had been one thing to talk ourselves into the cholera zone; it would be quite another thing to talk ourselves back out.

After praying for God's help and protection, I decided that I would attempt to walk past the guards and see what happened. They did not even seem to notice me. They never even looked at me as I walked right past them. No "Halt!" or "Where do you think you're going?"—nothing.

I started Heidi's Land Rover, drove into town and filled the back of the Land Rover with bottled water. Then I drove back to the hospital tent, again walked past the guards, found Heidi—who was still praying for and comforting the children—and told her that I had bought all the water I could find. The doctors were thrilled to hear that we had brought water and asked some of the guards to bring it in. What a relief it provided to those thirsty, suffering souls.

As we continued to pray, we saw miracle after miracle as people rose from their sick beds, healed, set free and filled with the love of Jesus. As the sick beds emptied, we began shipping the people back to their homes, while to others Heidi gave money to catch the local bus back to their families. What a miraculous and wonderful time that was.

By God's grace neither Heidi nor I came down with cholera. Many people lost their lives in that outbreak, but the image of Heidi putting herself at risk to meet the needs of others stays burned into my mind.

16

Never Shrink Back

*R*olland Baker is one tough fellow.

A grin spread across my face as I looked at the man walking next to me. Well, walking is not exactly the right word. We *had* been walking for more than five hours, and now we were trudging through the Muda River, sloshing through cold water up to our waists.

Several of us—five African pastors and Rolland—were on our way to the village of Nhamatanda to preach the Gospel. We planned to preach in several Mozambican villages that had been controlled by Renamo during the civil war. It was 1998 and the war had now been officially over for six years. In that time Renamo had transformed from a rebel army to a political party. But the memory of their devastating attack on Chico's village was still sharp and painful in my mind, and I was afraid of what we might find in these isolated villages; but first we had to get there. As we slogged our way through the swirling current, I wondered what creatures might accompany us in the water. Hungry crocodiles, perhaps? Bloodthirsty leeches, definitely.

When we had first reached the Muda, the other pastors wanted to carry Rolland across, but he flatly refused. Rolland Baker is an amazing man who will get right down on the same level with the people around him in order to share Jesus. In some of the villages we visited together, we were offered food that might be considered inedible by Western standards. Sometimes we were not even sure *what* we were eating, but I never saw Rolland turn away from anything. He would eat and drink anything that was put before him, because he knew it would make them more accepting of what he had to say about Jesus.

The first time I met Rolland, I thought he looked like a mild-mannered professor, with his distinguished-looking beard, his eyeglasses and his long, thin face. He had the appearance of the scholar that he is, but I was completely wrong to think of him as "mild mannered." It takes guts to spend your life on the mission field, and Rolland has plenty of those.

When Rolland rejected the offer to be carried across the Muda, the African-born pastors protested. They reminded him that they were accustomed to fording rivers like this one and that he was not. They did not think him weak, old or incapable; they merely wanted to show him the respect they felt was due him. Rolland would not buy it. The discussion was short; he insisted on carrying his own weight.

We had reached the riverbank now, and I winced as Rolland emerged from the water. Several huge black leeches about three inches long had fastened themselves onto the back of his right leg. The creatures were fat and full of their host's blood. I tapped him on the shoulder and pointed at the slimy bloodsuckers. "I'm afraid you've picked up some leeches."

"Oh well, no problem. Help me get them off."

His calm reaction surprised me. I had seen people cry and scream when they found leeches sucking their blood, and I did not blame them for it. I grabbed hold of one of the slippery worms and pulled. As I suspected it would, it stretched like a big piece of rubber. The harder I pulled, the deeper it dug into Rolland's leg. Rolland was likewise trying to remove one of the other leeches, with similar difficulty. I let go and sighed. "We'll have to burn them off," I said.

By God's grace we had a lighter, brought by another pastor for just such an occasion. He flicked it into action and put the flame next to the biggest leech, moving slowly and carefully to avoid burning Rolland. Almost immediately the creature withdrew and fell to the ground as blood streamed out of the wound it left behind. Then the man repeated the procedure to remove the other leeches. Within minutes Rolland's leg was bandaged, and we were back on the road. When one of the other pastors suggested that he might want to rest for a while, he brushed it off with characteristic good humor.

It was another hour or so before we finally reached the village. The desperation and poverty we found there defies description. The "clothes" the people wore were so ragged and tattered that it was impossible to tell whether they were worn-out trousers and shirts or the skins of goats or other animals. Some wore skirts made of nothing more than leaves or other plant fibers. We saw children with bellies swollen either from severe malnutrition or intestinal worms, and many adults were emaciated from chronic hunger. They had foods like bananas, mangoes and even some chickens, but they were malnourished because they were not getting a well-balanced diet with all of the vitamins and minerals they needed.

Word quickly spread that a group of strangers had arrived in the village, and almost everyone came out to meet us. But as soon as they saw Rolland, some of the younger children ran away screaming. They had never seen a white man before, and he terrified them. The adults were not afraid, but they were fascinated by his light-colored skin, and some of them wanted to touch it. He did not seem to mind.

When we talked to some of the leaders of the community, we discovered that they did not know the war was over and were afraid to leave their village. It had been six years since the cease-fire had been signed, and the very last of the violence had occurred two years later; but word of peace had yet to reach the people living in this Renamo-controlled district.

Before we left we gave them two great pieces of news: One, the war was finished, so they were free to travel and trade with other communities; and two, Jesus Christ had come to set them free from slavery to sin and death.

All the people in that community, or very nearly all, gave their lives to Christ that day. And, as is almost always the case in Africa, even though they were terribly poor, they insisted on giving us something in return. They presented us with mangoes and bananas and even offered us a chicken—which we declined as politely as possible, since the last thing we wanted to do was offend them.

Residents of the next village were just as happy to hear the good news of God's love. We had heard talk that the people living in this area were not receptive to the Gospel and would not listen to what we had to say. Instead we found them hungry for God and rejoicing to hear the good news that Jesus had come to save them. In some of the communities we visited, people came running to hear what we had to say. We took the Gospel into fifteen villages on that trip, and all of them welcomed us with open arms.

I took many such expeditions into the bush with Rolland. When we arrived in a new village, we often started by going into the fields where people were working. I would shout, "We are having a meeting and I have something to tell you." Or I might climb a tree and just start preaching in a loud voice. Sometimes Rolland preached and I translated his message into the Shona language; other times the preaching was left to me because my voice is naturally louder than his. After we got a battery-powered loudspeaker, our crowds got even bigger, and churches were planted in dozens of communities.

Checking on the Churches

Around this time I asked Rolland if he would accompany me on a visit to villages throughout northern Mozambique where I had planted churches. "I'd be happy to do that," he said. "How are the people in the churches getting along?"

"They are probably poor and hungry."

"Then we'll have to take some food with us." One of many things I have always appreciated about Rolland and Heidi Baker is that they care about people's physical needs as well as their spiritual needs. I have heard it said, "People don't care what you know until they know that you care." The Bakers care, and care deeply.

Traveling to the churches was a serious challenge. We drove through areas with no roads at all. If roads did exist, they were often little more than rutted, muddy trails that were better suited to oxcarts than modern vehicles. Once we were on our way to visit a church that had been started in the home of a railroad worker named Frank. As we passed the beach town of Xai-Xai, Rolland told us about a nearby mission base camp that he had known about for a long time but had never been able to go to, and he suggested that we pay a visit. We turned off the road to head to the beachside camp, and it was not long before we discovered that we had made a mistake. Our truck became stuck in the deep, soft sand, and we could not free it. The more we tried, the deeper our wheels sank into the soft soil.

Several men and boys came running from nearby huts to help us. They pushed, they pulled, they groaned and grunted, but the truck tires could not find traction in that sand. This went on for four hours, until one mighty, heroic, united shove jolted us out of the pit we had dug for ourselves. "Thank You, Jesus!" someone shouted. We thanked our helpers profusely, gave them a bag of rice for all their hard work and were back on our way—although quite a bit dirtier than before. We had sand in our hair, our clothes, our eyes—to say nothing of the perspiration that drenched us.

By this time we knew people were already waiting for us at Frank's house, but there was no way to let them know that we were delayed. An even bigger problem was that night was beginning to fall and we were still hours from our destination. It was not safe to travel after dark, so we had no choice but to stop for the night and continue our journey in the morning. We were going to arrive more than 24 hours later than we had planned.

As we drew near to our destination the following day, we were astonished to see a huge crowd still waiting for us at Frank's house. Hundreds of people stood in the yard, sat in trees, filled every possible space as they awaited our arrival. I was shocked by the multitude of people, especially since we were more than a day late. Obviously the church here was strong and healthy.

We drove the last 150 yards to Frank's house along a narrow, hard-packed dirt road flanked by rice paddies. In one place the road was too narrow for our truck. "Oh no!" Rolland suddenly moaned.

"'Oh no,' what?" I asked. Then I felt the back end of the vehicle sinking into the mud. "Oh," I sighed.

For the second time in as many days, we stuck fast and could not move. This time, though, we had hundreds of strong arms to help us. We were quickly surrounded by friends who pushed, pulled and struggled to free us, but sadly, they were fighting a losing battle. That swampy rice paddy proved a stronger foe than the sand. Even worse, the sky suddenly opened up and rain began to pour down.

Once again the battle continued for hours. We struggled in the rain while the women, who were also getting soaked by the rain, waited for us in Frank's yard, shivering in the cold while they lifted their voices in songs of praise. Finally some of the men went into the forest and cut some trees down to build a makeshift ramp we could use to escape the mud. It worked!

As you can see, holding camp meetings in the bush can present some difficult obstacles. By the time we got free, everyone was drenched, but we did not mind. We wound up having a great time in the Lord that day.

17

On Wings of Eagles

It looks beautiful from up here, doesn't it?" Rolland asked.

"Yes, it does," I replied, without shifting my gaze from the rolling green hills below. We were on our way to the city of Bangula in Iris Ministries' brand-new airplane. The countryside looked peaceful and beautiful as it passed beneath us. Baobab trees stretched their branches up toward the sky. Crystal clear lakes and ponds shimmered in the sun, surrounded by groups of thatched huts. We were looking down on the beauty of God's creation, too far away to see the hunger, poverty and need that that had been brought into the world by sin. I knew that down there, on the ground, people were suffering.

The year was 2001 and Mozambique was in the middle of a terrible drought. The hillsides were green, but no food crops were growing. The water looked clear, yet it was probably filled with bacteria and waterborne disease. The huts also looked beautiful from the air, but they were filled with hungry children and families. People were eating weeds, leaves, tree bark or anything else they could find that would fill their stomachs. I also knew that many of these people were trapped in spiritual darkness—they did

155

not know that God loved them or that He had sent Jesus to save their souls.

If you research Mozambique on the Internet, you will read that the country has a population of around 22 million people. I believe it is much higher than that. There are so many villages hidden in isolated jungles, far away from cities or major roads, and many of the people who live in them have never been counted.

We had spent many months traveling across Mozambique by foot and car, taking spiritual and physical nourishment to people in these remote areas. Often we had to drive for an entire day to reach a small community of a few hundred people. We began praying that God would give us a better, more efficient way to reach them. I could not stand the thought that people were dying and going into hell because it was taking us so long to reach their villages with the Good News.

God answered those prayers by giving Iris Ministries the small bush airplane in which we were now riding. In an airplane we could travel from one end of Mozambique to the other in a few hours instead of several days. We could now do in one week what had taken us three to accomplish before. All we had to do was find a flat piece of ground, one where goats were not grazing, that we could use as a landing strip.

One of our earliest trips by air had taken us to the village of Marromeu. As our pilot circled the village looking for a good place to land, hundreds of people poured out of their homes and began running across the fields beneath us, yelling and waving their arms in greeting. The arrival of our tiny plane was obviously a huge event in Marromeu; as soon as we landed, we were surrounded by hundreds of people who wanted to see the airplane and hear why we had come. All we had to do was stand in the door of the plane and begin preaching.

The same thing happened at our next stop, Shipanga. In fact, so many people crowded around us in that village that I had to climb into a tree to preach! Everywhere we went hundreds, even thousands, of people came to hear what we had to say. The airplane was not only an efficient method of transportation, it was also a wonderful means of drawing a crowd.

We could not do the same thing in Bangula, however, where the situation of its people was especially desperate, not only because of the drought but because it is situated in one of the poorest areas of Mozambique. There we had to land some distance from the city and hire a car to drive us to the location where we planned to preach. Not only did the people not see or hear our approach, but nobody even knew we were coming—we had not been able to communicate with any of the pastors of the churches God used me to plant in the area. Yet, when we reached the spot where we planned to preach, we were surprised and delighted to find a large crowd waiting for us.

As we stepped out of our vehicle, Pastor Nsbe, a wonderful man of faith, stepped forward to welcome us. This dear man lost all five of his children to hunger and disease, and afterward opened his heart and his home to eight orphaned children who had no one to care for them. In his deep, booming voice he said, "Welcome, brothers! We have been waiting for you."

My mind raced back to the day Mr. Lukas met Gafar and me coming out of the jungle. "But how did you know we were coming?" I asked.

"We saw it in a dream," he answered.

"We?" I asked.

"Yes." He smiled. I looked around and saw many other familiar faces, men who had first heard about God's love from me and who were now leading congregations in their communities. We were amazed to discover that all of these pastors had the same dream and had come to meet us independently of one another. It was only after they arrived that they discovered the others had also been called in a dream. And they were not the only ones who had been called this way. As we ministered that day, one person after another told us that they had learned in a dream that we were coming. We enjoyed a wonderful time of celebration together, and many souls were won for God's kingdom.

How to Have a Good Day

Another time we traveled to Malawi to minister in a village called Nsanje. We planned to get there around midmorning but were unable to fly into the area, and because the roads were so bad, we did not arrive until midafternoon. Once again we discovered that about five hundred people had been waiting for us all day, gathered under a group of trees near the community school to hear what we had to say. As was almost always the case in these relatively isolated, rural areas of Malawi, people were desperately poor. They were ragged and thin and had almost nothing in the way of worldly possessions. They had been poor to begin with, and the drought that had Malawi in its grasp had pushed them to the edge of starvation.

All morning I had expected Rolland to preach, but as the service was about to begin, he turned to me and asked if I would give the sermon that day. I had no subject in mind, but when I asked God what He wanted me to share with His people, I felt very strongly that He wanted me to encourage them. As I looked out at those weary, sad faces waiting for something they could grab hold of, God gave me the topic I was to speak on: *How to have a good day.*

I asked them what they considered to be a good day. "Some people," I said, "live in cities and work a whole year to earn enough money to take a trip to the bush. To them, a good day is time spent in a village like this one. Other people who live in the bush work all year to make enough money to go into town to shop. They think visiting a town is a good day."

I told them they did not have to wait all year to have a good day, nor did they have to have nice clothes and big homes to have a good day. "The Bible talks about people who had everything a person can own, and they still didn't have a good day. A good day is one when you are at peace. If you have peace inside you, you will have a good day. If you find Jesus, you will have peace." As I shared the Gospel, waves of energy seemed to ripple through the crowd. People were nodding in agreement, smiling, laughing and joyfully slapping each other on the back, becoming refreshed and restored as I spoke.

"We have come here to encourage you in this time of famine," I said. "I want you to know, you need Jesus to have a good day. There are people in the city of Blantyre who have good homes and plenty of food and clothes, and they still don't have a good day. If you have Jesus in your life, you'll find yourself laughing in the middle of the night even if mice come into your home and start nibbling on your toes." People began to laugh at the idea of lying there giggling while mice chewed on their toes. "You'll have a big smile on your face, even if cockroaches are crawling over you and biting the palms of your hands."

A woman near the front of the crowd began to shake as she tried to stifle the laughter that was building up inside of her. She put her hand over her mouth, but it did not help; soon she was doubled over. Immediately two men on either side of her began to laugh uncontrollably. Laughter quickly spread through the crowd like a fire being passed from one candle to another. Within minutes all the people were laughing with the joy of the Lord. It was wonderful to witness this joy spreading through the crowd and refreshing His people.

The Devil Hates Laughter

True joy is a great weapon against the devil. Because of this, and because of what Jesus did for me, I laugh a lot. One time a well-meaning friend told me that I needed to be more serious. "More serious?" I asked.

"Yes. You laugh too much."

I smiled back at him. "I can't help it. Jesus makes me happy."

"But if you're laughing all the time, people won't respect you," he protested. That may or may not be true, but I know that Satan will respect me and flee, and that is what I want.

I once joined some pastors who were having a terrible time trying to free a man from demonic possession. The man had kicked, hit and spit as they tried to drive the demon out. When we commanded the demon to leave in the name of Jesus, he swore at us and struggled even more.

"I cast you out in the name of Jesus Christ!" I shouted.

The man glared at me, his lips twisted into a hateful sneer. "I won't go."

"In the name of Jesus . . ." I began again.

"No!" he screamed, spitting in my direction. "You get out!" He again began to curse and swear, telling us all the terrible things he was going to do to us. In the midst of the chaos and confusion, I heard God speak to my heart: *Laugh.*

"Lord?"

I want you to laugh.

And so I laughed. My friends looked at me as if I had lost my mind.

"Ha, ha, ha, ha!" I continued to laugh, motioning for my friends to join me. I could see they were not getting it, so I began to laugh harder. The demonized man put his hands over his ears and yelled for me to be quiet. My friends' eyes lit up at his reaction, and they began to laugh along with me. As they did the demon drove the man to his knees, let out an ear-splitting shriek and was gone. The joy of the Lord had brought deliverance when we felt like giving up.

Another important revelation about the value of being joyful came to me at a church I visited in Malawi. The service had been lovely, with wonderful songs and a powerful sermon. Then the pastor told everyone to get down on their knees. As they knelt all around me, people began to weep and moan loudly. I did not want to do anything to disrupt the service, so I knelt down with them and began thinking about the cross and all that Jesus had suffered there. But instead of crying, I began to laugh.

I tried to hold it in, but it was no use. The laughter was trying to explode out of me, and I could not control myself. While people all around me were crying their eyes out, I rolled on the floor laughing until I could no longer catch my breath. I would have been terribly embarrassed, but the anointing was strong and I simply could not stop.

When the service ended, the pastor took me aside and asked me why I had been laughing like that. "Pastor," I said, "I tried to cry. I really did. But the Lord wiped away my tears and made me laugh."

One Good Day after Another

The Lord wiped away the tears of the people of Nsanje that day. They were tired, hungry and poor and desperately needed to be refreshed in body, mind and spirit. God gave them refreshment in the form of laughter.

We laughed and laughed and laughed . . . and then we laughed some more. As we laughed I felt in my spirit that the demons that had caused so much trouble for those dear people were fleeing in terror. I believe that Satan cannot bear to hear the sound of God's people laughing. Godly joy is one of our greatest weapons.

After the service ended we discovered that the people had not had anything to eat all day, so Rolland and I went to the market and bought cornmeal for everyone. For many of them the food we provided was all that stood between them and starvation.

Ever since that day one of the first things Rolland says to me whenever I see him is, "Are you having a good day?"

My answer is always yes. I'm always having a great day. How could it be anything else when I belong to Jesus!

18

Culture Shock

I spent most of those years on the road, sometimes with Rolland, Heidi or other missionaries, other times by myself. I crisscrossed southern Africa, through Mozambique, Malawi, South Africa, Tanzania, Kenya, Zambia and other countries in the region. When I was not visiting churches I had already planted, I was busy planting new ones.

I found that, through God's great power and grace, none of the churches He had allowed me to plant had fallen away from the faith. They were all strong, growing and full of the Spirit. I take no credit for this. I just know that God is faithful; when we look to Him, He sustains and guides. All of these churches rejoiced to hear about my work for Iris Ministries and were happy to extend the right hand of fellowship.

I had no idea, however, that God was about to take me out of Africa to send me around the world! In 2001 I was invited to the United States to share at Bethel School of Supernatural Ministry in Redding, California. Ten years later, I have traveled millions of miles and visited nearly every country in the world. I speak seventeen different languages and have learned to be at peace in any culture. But it was not always so.

When I received the invitation to Bethel Church, I had never left Africa before, so you can imagine my shock when I arrived at the airport in San Francisco. My eyes could not believe what I was seeing: The skyscrapers, the hundreds of airplanes flying this way and that like birds, the speed that people drove in their cars, which were everywhere—all of it amazed me. On the one hand I was excited, and on the other I was completely astonished and a little afraid. When I got off the airplane, I wanted to get down on my knees and kiss the soil, but I could not find anything but concrete, and it does not help to kiss the concrete. So I just followed the crowds through the labyrinthine airport passageways toward immigration.

When I handed the official my passport, I could not understand a word he was saying because I was completely overwhelmed. Thank God that at that time there were far fewer questions than they ask today—good news for me! Even simple things like Coca-Cola coming out of a tap seemed astounding. It still amazes me that God reached down to a remote, poor village and chose me to share His Word with people all over the world—but He did!

Freezing in Toronto

The following year I was invited to speak at a conference in Toronto, Canada. It was October, and I have never been so cold in my life. My hosts did not think it was that cold. They told me that Toronto is a lot colder in January and February. When I heard that I asked God, "Please don't ever send me to Toronto in January or February."

I had a wonderful time in Canada despite the initial concern that I might freeze to death! One evening I was in a session at the conference when I suddenly had a vision of the angels dancing in harmony. I was enraptured by the beautiful spectacle, unaware of anything else around me as I watched

164

hundreds of angels form a line and split into a number of different formations. They wore silk robes that sparkled as they stretched out their wings. I was enthralled by the grace, precision and energy of the angels' movements; I could have watched them dance for hours.

Actually, that is what I did. When the vision faded, I discovered that I was lying on the floor in an empty conference room. Nobody must have noticed me lying there when the session ended. I struggled to my feet and made my way to the door, feeling giddy and a bit clumsy—not unlike someone who has had a bit too much to drink. It reminded me of Paul's words to the Ephesians: "Do not get drunk on wine, which leads to debauchery. Instead, be filled with the Spirit, speaking to one another with psalms, hymns, and songs from the Spirit" (Ephesians 5:18–19).

All the doors to the conference room were shut, but if I wanted to leave, I had no choice but to go through one of them. As soon as I did, a siren wailed in protest. I walked out and shut the door, but the alarm kept blasting in my ears. Even worse, a man in uniform came running down the hall in my direction. I smiled and hoped he would know that I was not a troublemaker; I had a feeling that he would not understand that I had been in the locked room because I had been watching angels dancing! By God's grace the guard was a pleasant fellow who kept telling me, "Don't worry about it. These things happen."

A Fireball in Michigan

My next stop was Michigan, where I stayed in the house of an attorney named Harry Hudson. It was past midnight when I finished visiting with my hosts and went up to the room that had been prepared for me. Just as I was getting into bed, a man walked into the room. I did not know for certain who he was, but I felt sure that I had met him before. As I opened my mouth to greet him, he reached out and took my hands into his and held them very tightly. Immediately something like a fireball exploded in front of me, and the man disappeared in the blinding light.

I found that I was crying uncontrollably. I also was burning hot and sweating like I had just run a mile in the African sun. I looked around me and noticed that the bedclothes had been torn apart, with the blanket and sheets lying in a heap on the floor. I felt completely exhausted, too weak even to make the bed, so I slept without covers. Actually, I slept very little that night.

I still do not know who the man was or what the experience meant, but it had a powerful effect on me.

Praying for Jim Goll

On to the Nashville, Tennessee, area, where I spoke at Grace Center. The pastor there, Brian Smallwood, asked me if I would pray for Jim Goll, a dear friend and leader in the congregation who was battling cancer. "He has to leave tomorrow for a trip to the West Coast, and he really needs a touch from the Lord," Brian told me.

Though I had not met Jim, I had heard of him and his prophetic ministry, and I was happy and honored to pray for him. We met in the soaking room at Grace Center, and I laid my hand on his chest and began to pray. After a minute or two he began to tremble noticeably. "Fire!" he shouted. "Hot fire!" He pulled away from me as if my hands were burning hot.

We knew that God had moved in a mighty way. We both left town immediately after that, so I did not get any news for a few weeks. Then I received an email telling me that Brother Goll had gone to see his doctor for a checkup, and the cancer was gone.

He stayed in remission for three years before the cancer returned. Thankfully, as I write this he is once again free from cancer. What a battler and a wonderful man of faith!

Laughter in London

Shortly after this I made my first trip to London. When I got off the plane, I was laughing and praising the Lord as I made my way to immigration. At the immigration desk, the government official gave me a cold stare. He gazed down at my passport for a long time before looking back up at me. "Who are you traveling with?" he asked.

"No one," I said. "I came by myself."

He wrinkled his brow as if he did not believe me. "Then why were you laughing like that?"

"Laughing?"

He nodded toward a small television monitor in his booth. "You were laughing as you came up the hall," he said. "What was so funny?"

I had no idea that I was being watched from the moment I got off the plane, so I felt a little embarrassed. But I remember thinking that I have a God who is so gracious to have brought me there. After a few more questions, the man let me through. I was still laughing in my heart but made up my mind that I would not let it show on my face. At least not until I was out of the airport.

Tsunami!

In August 2004 I was at Ekukhanyeni Christian Retreat in South Africa where we were holding one of our regular advanced conferences for pastors. The village of Ekukhanyeni was surrounded by mountains about 2,000 feet high, and on the last day, as we came out of the retreat center, I suddenly saw huge waves of water cascading over the mountaintops. A flood of unimaginable size and power was headed straight for us. The pictures were so vivid that I started shouting, "Tsunami! Tsunami! Tsunami!" The people with me cried back, "What tsunami? Where? What's going on?" When I looked again the visions had stopped.

A missionary named Brenda suggested that I was seeing a tsunami of the Holy Spirit, and I agreed that perhaps it was. Three months later we held a conference in Pemba, and once again, right in the middle of the conference, I began seeing tsunamis. This time the waves were crashing over many islands with devastating force. A voice in my ear urged me to prophesy life over these islands, so I did. Soon I began to feel an urgency about going to India and applied for a visa. My passport was returned to me with the date December 24, 2004, stamped on the last blank page.

As you probably remember, on December 26 the worst tsunami in recorded history stormed across Indonesia and into India, Thailand and Sri Lanka, sweeping more than 200,000 people to their deaths. I stood in shock as I watched accounts of the disaster on television, and I realized that I had seen all of it before—in the visions. I cried out, "Oh, Lord, You tried to warn me!" If I had clearly understood what God was telling me, I could have issued a warning that might have saved thousands of lives. But I did not understand.

As I watched the tragic scene unfolding, God gently reminded me that I had been faithful in prophesying life to these devastated islands. For that reason, I feel certain that, although thousands were killed, God intervened to save the lives of many thousands more who otherwise would have perished. I also believe that many of those who died were drawn to Christ in the days before the disaster. They are now alive with Him, in heaven, forever.

I left for India a few days later to help in the rescue effort.

Before I move on, I want to say a few more words about the tsunami. I do not believe for one minute that God sent this disaster. Terrible things like this happen because God's people have not taken dominion over nature, as God instructed us to do (see Genesis 1:26, 28; in the King James Version of the Bible, it reads, "Let [man] have dominion . . . over all the earth"). As a result, nature is in rebellion and we experience terrible earthquakes, floods, cyclones and hurricanes.

I also believe that the Lord does not allow anything of this magnitude to take place without first revealing it to His people. Nothing comes without warning; God is always telling us what will happen in the days to come, but we must listen and pray for understanding.

The Bible tells that "even the winds and the waves" obeyed our Lord's commands (Matthew 8:27). Jesus said, "Very truly I tell you, whoever believes in me will do the works I have been doing, and they will do even greater things than these, because I am going to the Father" (John 14:12). God expects us to stand on His Word and grab hold of the authority He has given us.

I experienced this authority years ago when I was staying in Beira with Tom, the railway worker who had begun holding meetings in his home. A group of us had gathered under a huge tree in order to hold a crusade, and a terrible storm was about to overrun us. The storm would have prevented us from sharing Jesus with all the people who had come to listen, so the leaders came together to stand on God's Word and pray. As we prayed, the storm ended and the sun started shining.

More recently, we received news in Pemba of an approaching tsunami that was due to hit at 11:15 that night. We began interceding and praying, continuing through to midnight. We later heard reports that a second huge wave hit the tsunami, causing it to turn back on itself. In August 2011, I was in Cape Town, where there was a severe drought. At a meeting the farmers asked me to pray for rain; that Friday night the rain started falling.

It is written in the Bible that we have authority over the earth, but we cannot use this authority without faith. With faith we can move anything that comes against us; Jesus Himself said that we can even move a mountain. But we must take up our faith in order to take up our authority.

19

Martyred for the Gospel

I know that fellow from somewhere. But where?

He was a pleasant-looking man, a few years older than I was. He was waiting in line to shake my hand after I delivered a Sunday-morning sermon at a church in Dondo, Mozambique. I could tell by the big smile on his face that he thought he knew me, but as hard as I tried, I could not place him.

Now we were face-to-face. He took my hand into both of his. "Surprise, it's your cousin Ezekiel."

"Ezekiel! My brother!" I shouted. We embraced as I cried, "God is so good!"

"Amen!" he agreed. "I have been hearing so many good things about you."

I shook my head in wonder. "But how did you . . . ? Where do you . . . ?" I could not ask the million questions that swirled around my head fast enough.

"I'm serving the Lord, too," he said.

I had not seen Ezekiel since before I left my parents' house. When we were growing up, I considered him my brother, because my parents had raised him and his sister Bulena after their mother, my aunt, died. Bulena, who

171

was quite a bit older, had married and moved away when I was still a boy. Ezekiel had eventually gone off to make his way in the world, and we had completely lost contact with each other.

"I heard about all the wonderful things God is doing through this person named Surprise," he said. "I had to come see for myself if they were talking about you . . . and now I know they were." He went on to tell me that after he left Mozambique, he made his way to Zambia. There he heard the Gospel at a Christian Reformed Church and accepted Christ. He had gone on to become a leader in that church; then he had returned to Mozambique, where he was serving as an evangelist and pastor. My heart overflowed with joy. How wonderful to have this reunion with Ezekiel and discover that in addition to being my blood relative, he was also my brother in Christ.

He drove me to his house in the nearby town of Manga and introduced me to his wife, Rita, and their children. It added to my joy to know that he and Rita were people of great compassion who had taken a number of orphaned children into their home. We had a wonderful day getting reacquainted with each other and worshiping the Lord together. Then we all went back for the evening service in Dondo.

Over the next year he came to White River twice for short visits with Tryphina and me. We laughed over old memories and praised God for all He had done in our lives. We had a very happy time together. But late one afternoon during his second visit, he suddenly became quiet. He cleared his throat and I leaned closer, expecting him to say something important.

He hesitated and cleared his throat again. "I wanted to tell you . . . some people have told me to stop preaching."

I sat straight up. "What people?"

He explained that he had been told that some people of another faith did not approve of his evangelism. "They told me that if I don't stop telling everyone about Jesus . . . they're going to kill me."

"Kill you?" I repeated. "Have you told the police?"

He shook his head. "That wouldn't do any good."

"What are you going to do?" I asked, even though I already knew what his answer would be.

He smiled and shrugged. "I'm going to keep on preaching. What else can I do?"

We sat in silence for a moment, and then he said, "I'm only telling you about it so you'll know if anything happens."

When I asked for the details, he told me that he had been accosted by a group of young men after preaching in the local market. They slapped him around a bit and told him the preaching had to stop . . . or else. "My brother," I said, "our lives are in the hands of God. Let us trust Him completely in this matter."

"Yes, yes!" he agreed.

"We need to forgive them completely, and pray for them, that they might come to know the love of Jesus."

"I have forgiven them, and I have been praying for them," Ezekiel replied. We knelt down immediately and asked the Lord to pour out His grace and mercy on these lost souls, to draw them to Himself. I knew that Ezekiel was not worried about himself; he was ready for whatever the Lord had planned for him. But he was a committed family man who deeply loved his wife and children and was concerned about what would happen to them if he was taken from them.

Over the next several months, Ezekiel kept on preaching. Wherever he went, he shared about Jesus—on the train, on the bus, in the market, everywhere. But when I had an opportunity to visit him in Mozambique, he told me that he had been attacked and threatened again. His foes had knocked him down and kicked him, leaving bruises but no serious injuries. He was rejoicing that Jesus had counted him worthy to suffer for the Gospel.

Then, on September 25, 2007, I woke up feeling as if I had been beaten to within an inch of my life. I was in terrible pain from head to toe and could not understand what had happened to me. I spent that entire day in the grip of the most horrible pain I had ever felt.

Night was just falling when the telephone rang. "Is this Uncle Surprise?" asked a shaky voice.

"Yes, it is."

"It's Janja." Janja was a young man who had been taken in by Ezekiel and Rita, and it was very unusual for him to telephone us.

"Hello, Janja," I said. "Is everything all right?"

"I have something to tell you about your brother Ezekiel," he said. "It's a sad story . . . he is no longer living."

"What did you say?" I asked, hoping I had misunderstood him.

"He is no longer living," Janja repeated. "He was murdered last night."

"What?"

"He was walking back to Manga after preaching in downtown Beira when he was attacked and killed." Janja paused for a moment. "He had been receiving threats."

"Yes, I know." He went on to tell me that Ezekiel had been beaten and stabbed so viciously that he was not recognizable. His attackers had cut off his lips and his tongue to show that they had killed him because of the things he had said. The rest of his body had been mutilated as well.

"The police didn't find him until this morning," he said. "They were able to identify him only because of his Bible." I thanked Janja for calling me and told him I would come to Mozambique as soon as I could.

As I hung up the phone, the physical pain left me. Suddenly, I felt fine. That was when I knew that God had allowed me to feel the pain Ezekiel had endured as he was being killed. I do not know why, but God allowed me to share in the sufferings of my cousin. It brought to me the reality of Jesus' suffering when He carried upon His own body the penalty for my sins:

> Surely he took up our pain and bore our suffering, yet we considered him punished by God, stricken by him, and afflicted. But he was pierced for our transgressions, he was crushed for our iniquities; the punishment that brought us peace was on him, and by his wounds we are healed. We all, like sheep, have gone astray, each of us has turned to our own way; and the LORD has laid on him the iniquity of us all.
>
> Isaiah 53:4–6

I also came to understand through this that much of the pain we feel is spiritual pain. Doctors and medicine are wonderful gifts from God, but often healing will come through drawing closer to God.

A few days later I had the privilege of delivering the eulogy at Ezekiel's funeral. Thousands of people came to show their love and respect for him, and many responded when I shared the Gospel. Ezekiel's killers had meant to silence him, but they had done just the opposite: In death he became an even more powerful witness for Christ.

I do not know why Ezekiel was not delivered from the hands of those who took his life. All I can say about this is that God always knows what is best. God has His purposes, and His ways are not our ways. No matter what happens, we have to keep pressing on and never give up, for our obedience is so very important. When hard times hit us, we need to focus on what God is doing, and not on what He is not doing. This helps keep our faith strong and helps us through the difficult times.

When hard times hit us, we need to focus on what God is doing and not on what He is not—that helps keep our faith strong to get through these difficult times. I have seen many miracles in similar situations. Late one night during a women's conference, I received word that one of our church's pastors had been beaten and stabbed to death. Apparently he had gone back to lock up the building when gang members attacked him. I immediately felt that God was calling me to prayer—for the young men who had killed my friend.

Later, as our pastor was being dropped off at the morgue in a body bag, he began moving around. He was alive, although his face was badly bruised and swollen. Within a matter of hours he was completely restored—not a mark on him! He was perfectly fine and anxious to go home, except that he was naked under the blue sheet. (The police had taken his clothes, as is customary with a murder victim.) I had to go out and buy him a shirt and some trousers. The young man who had delivered the fatal blow was arrested and put in jail. When he saw how his "victim" had been restored, he surrendered his life to Jesus.

In early August 2005, I was very nearly killed. I traveled to Sudan to hold a series of Gospel meetings with Pastor James, a very tall, elderly pastor from the south of the country. Sudan was going through a terror very similar to what Mozambique had experienced years earlier: a long and brutal civil war. In southern Sudan more than two million people had been killed between 1983 and 2005, and more than four million had fled from their homes, many taking refuge in crowded, desperately poor refugee camps.

In January 2005, after more than twenty years of fighting, a truce was signed between the government and the Sudan People's Liberation Army, which was headed by a charismatic leader named John Garang. A few weeks prior to my trip to Sudan, Garang had been sworn in as vice president of the coalition government. Then Garang was killed in a helicopter crash while returning from Uganda. The Sudanese government blamed the crash on bad weather, but many felt that sabotage was involved, and riots broke out across the country. More than twenty people were killed in Khartoum alone.

The day after John Garang's death, Pastor James and I preached in a refugee camp, completely unaware of what was happening elsewhere in the country. We had a wonderful time, and many accepted Jesus as their Lord and Savior. After our meeting we boarded a bus for Khartoum. The day was clear, bright and, as is often the case in Sudan, scorching hot. As we approached the outskirts of the capital city, we suddenly saw huge flames billowing ahead of us. The next thing we knew we were surrounded by a wild and angry mob carrying machetes and spears. Some ran in front of us, forcing our driver to stomp on the brakes. The bus fishtailed, turning almost completely around, and some began beating on the sides of the vehicle.

I looked out of the window and saw a mass of angry people fighting with each other. Some continued to fight even when blood started pouring down their faces. Others lay in the street, severely injured. People were being killed and wounded right in front of us. The scene was complete confusion and carnage as the rioters shouted at each other. They had set fire to the petrol station, vehicles, homes and houses.

"Everybody out!" our driver yelled as he ran down the steps and disappeared into the chaos. He had not even set the brake, and the bus continued to roll forward. I heard the sound of shattering glass as rioters began breaking the windows, spraying jagged shards onto the frightened passengers. All around us people were desperately trying to get off the bus. Some climbed through broken windows and jumped to the ground, injuring themselves as they fell.

Pastor James and I managed to jump through our window without hurting ourselves, and we fled down the street. I clutched my large Bible as I ran. Pastor James shouted at me, "Drop the Bible! Drop the Bible!" I knew what he was trying to say. I could run faster without that big Bible, but I did not want to let it go.

I fled eastward, past burning houses, through hundreds of people running in every direction. I ran for my life, my heart pumping and pounding, knowing I could be killed at any moment. I came around a corner and was suddenly face-to-face with a huge mob armed with machetes and spears. My heart was overwhelmed. I was running as fast as I could go, and they were almost upon me. There was no way I could turn back or get away. I was going to die.

"Lord," I cried, "please take care of Tryphina and our boys."

I held my Bible against my chest and closed my eyes, preparing to be engulfed by the massive sea of rioters. I tensed as I waited for the pain of a machete slicing through my body. I cannot describe the horror of that moment.

Immediately, everything became quiet.

What happened? Was I dead?

I opened my eyes and looked around. Everything was peaceful and quiet. I was standing on the veranda of the Acropole Hotel in downtown Khartoum. I had no idea how I got there. Dazed, I went inside and saw people relaxing over coffee and tea, acting as if nothing at all were wrong.

The next thing I did was call Pastor James on my cell phone. I feared the worst, as he was an elderly gentleman who used a walking stick to get around. Miraculously, he, too, had survived, although he was still miles away on the other side of the city.

I cannot explain what happened to me except to say that I was supernaturally transported like Philip the Evangelist (see Acts 8:39). I believe what the Bible says in Psalm 91: God will send His angels to help His people when we are in danger. According to His promise, He will not let us fall; He will stretch out his hand to pick us up.

We must never stop trusting the Lord. When we are weak, He is strong. When we sleep, He never slumbers. He is always at work watching over those who love Him.

20

Adventure in Backdoor

After years in White River, Tryphina and I both felt that the Lord was calling us to move to the town of Backdoor. At the time Backdoor was a good place to stay away from. It was known as the roughest town in our district, a place where gangs ran wild, drug use was rampant and violence was common.

When I told friends that we planned to move there, they begged us not to go. "God has plenty of work for you to do right here," one of them said. "Why would you want to go to a place like that?"

"Because God is calling us," I answered.

"But you have children. Think about their safety." At the time, Enoch and Lovey were small, and Tryphina was well along in her pregnancy with Israel.

"We have spent a great deal of time praying about this," I said. "We both feel that God is calling us to show His love to the people of Backdoor. He will protect the children." Tryphina and I both wanted to make a difference in a place where people were afraid to go into the streets at night, where they lived in constant fear from criminals who had shown again and again that they had no respect for human life.

I remembered how, years earlier, I had been warned not to go back to Mozambique. Those who had warned me were correct in their judgment of the situation. I experienced many horrible situations, but God had protected me through them all. And I believed He would continue to protect us now.

It was not long before my belief was put to a severe test. Before we even moved into our new home, thieves broke in and stole some of the things we had stored there. Among the items taken were the walkie-talkies that our ministry teams used to communicate when we traveled into rural areas.

A couple of days later Tryphina, Lovey and I were taking a walk in our new neighborhood. As we passed an old, dilapidated house down the street from where we lived, we heard the unmistakable sound of someone speaking through a walkie-talkie.

I probably should have let it go, or called the police. Instead I decided to see for myself who had stolen our equipment. I stepped around to the side of the house and spied a young man holding one of the walkie-talkies. When he saw that I had spotted him, he ran into the house. Suddenly a group of wild-eyed men, armed with long machetes and a gun, burst out of the house and ran toward me.

"Run!" I shouted to Tryphina. "Run!"

I scooped Lovey into my arms, and we raced for home as fast as our legs would carry us. "Stop them!" one of the men shouted. "Kill them!"

I did not know for sure how many of them there were—seven or eight at least, and they were right on our heels. It was uphill all the way to our house, and there was no way we could outrun them.

"There!" Tryphina shouted, pointing at a nearby house. We ran to the front door, praying that it would be unlocked.

It was!

We scrambled inside, slammed the door just in front of our pursuers and fumbled to lock it before they could follow us inside. Our hearts were pounding in our chests as the thieves began banging on the door. "You're dead meat!" one of them screamed. "We're going to kill you!"

As they shouted and banged on the door outside, we heard a harsh voice behind us. "What are you doing in my house?" We turned to see an angry-looking man in a wheelchair.

"They're trying to kill us," I said.

"Get out of here," he snarled.

"Didn't you hear me?" I asked. "We can't go out there. They'll kill us." Two gunshots sounded outside as if to emphasize what I was saying. I hoped they were shooting into the air.

The man's angry expression remained fixed. "I'm going to open this door," he said. He tried to move his wheelchair toward the door, but I reached out and blocked him as Tryphina pushed up against the door, trying to make certain it stayed shut.

Outside, neighbors had gathered to see what was going on, but no one seemed inclined to help us. They might as well have been watching a football game. "What's happening?" I heard someone ask.

"I think they're killing some people."

"Oh."

I fumbled in my pocket, found my cell phone and pressed the number of a pastor I knew, praying that he would answer.

He did. "It's Surprise," I shouted into the phone. "We need the police. Quick!" I told him where we were, hung up and prayed that God would protect us until the police got there. Finally, after about fifteen minutes, we heard the sound of sirens in the distance, and we knew the police were on their way.

It was only after they got everything under control that we discovered why the man in the wheelchair had been so angry. He was actually the leader of the gang that had broken into our house. He was in a wheelchair because he had been wounded in a previous shootout with the police. This time, his gang gave up without a fight. Through God's grace, not only were the robbers arrested, but our possessions were returned to us.

After what had happened, our friends again begged us to change our minds and stay in White River, but we knew we had to follow through on what God had told us to do. We moved into our new home early in 2004, and Israel was born a few weeks later.

As soon as we moved into our new house, we began reaching out to our neighbors with God's love, and as they responded, the community began to change. We also began taking in orphaned children and homeless people who had nowhere else to go. When people saw that we lived in a way that was consistent with what we said, they wanted to know more about our faith, and many of them came into the Kingdom.

Gradually people who had been intimidated by the criminals began to speak out for a better community. There was still a lot of violence in Backdoor, but it was mainly criminals killing criminals, until the gangs had all but disappeared.

Over time the atmosphere of the village became peaceful and sweet. Missionaries are being sent from there. Local Christians are caring for children who have lost their parents to AIDS or crime. The light of God's love is shining brightly.

Lovey and the Water Tank

God performed many miracles during this time, including one that involved Lovey and Israel. One afternoon I was lying on my bed reading while Israel, who was just one month old, lay in his crib near my bed. I sensed that someone had come into the room, and I looked up to see Lovey standing next to the bed.

"Dad, let's pray."

"All right," I said. "Do you want to pray here?"

"Let's go into the kitchen."

I got up and took his hand, and we walked together into the kitchen, where Tryphina was fixing dinner. "Lovey wants to pray," I explained.

She smiled that loving smile only a mom can give, and then she asked, "Where is Israel?"

"He's in his crib," I said. "He'll be fine."

Her brow wrinkled. "I think I'll go get him."

"But he's really fine," I said.

"I'd feel better if he was in here with us," she replied. She retreated into the bedroom and returned carrying Israel wrapped in a blanket. Almost immediately, a terrifying crash sounded from that part of the house.

We rushed in to find that the five-hundred-liter tank that provided water for the house had toppled over and crashed straight through the bedroom wall. Its shattered remains lay across the crib where Israel had been sleeping, and on the bed where I had been resting just a few minutes earlier. If we had stayed in the room, we would have been killed.

When I think about how many times the Lord has rescued me out of impossible situations, I marvel at His faithfulness. I think of how He rescued me from the jungle, protected me from death amongst the terrors of war and transported me from certain death in Sudan. He provided me supernaturally with seventeen languages, guided me from place to place, gave me such a wonderful family and used me powerfully to bring hope to a dark world, and I am filled with joy. As I sit surrounded by my boys, Enoch, Lovey, Israel and Blessing, He remains my best friend, my hope, my very life, and I am filled with the desire to tell all those that do not know just how great a God He is.

21

Visions of Tomorrow

What I have told you is really just the beginning of my adventure. There is so much more to tell—and perhaps some of it will find its way into another book, if that is what the Lord wants.

My purpose in writing is twofold: First, I want to encourage you to be strong in your faith by sharing with you what God is able to do through an ordinary man who trusts and believes in Him. If I thought for a moment that this book was about Surprise Sithole, I never would have agreed to write it. But it is not about me; it is about God! I wanted to share with you His faithfulness, His power and His amazing love.

My second purpose in writing this book—and really, the most important reason—is to share the Gospel of Jesus Christ. John 3:16 says, "For God so loved the world that he gave his one and only Son, that whoever believes in him shall not perish but have eternal life." If you have not yet accepted God's Son, Jesus, as your Lord and Savior, please do it right now. Simply ask Him to take your sins away and He will. He died on the cross to pay the penalty for our sins, He was buried and He rose on the third day so that we might live forever with Him in heaven. He offers you the free gift of eternal life. All you have to do is accept it!

Jesus Is Coming Soon!

Today revival continues to spread throughout Africa.

Through the work of Iris Ministries, thousands upon thousands of people have been set free from the bondage imposed by counterfeit spirituality and have stepped into the freedom of a relationship with Christ. Churches are being established almost every day, and existing congregations are growing in numbers and spiritual strength.

Many who have come to know Jesus through Iris Ministries are traveling from village to village preaching the Gospel. We are taking tent crusades into many areas, where God is using us to heal the sick, cast out demons and feed and care for orphaned children and widows in the name of Jesus. Bible schools have been established in several cities. Everywhere I go, I discover that people are hungry for more of God. As Jesus said, "Open your eyes and look at the fields! They are ripe for harvest" (John 4:35). Much has been accomplished, but so much remains to be done.

In Malawi our goal was to start a church in every village. The last time I checked, we had started more than a thousand churches in that country along with a Bible school. All the students in that Bible school are going out into the bush and planting churches every week.

In 1998 Iris Ministries started holding conferences in Mozambique, where the leaders of the village churches could come for spiritual nurture and training. These conferences have had a tremendous impact. Pastors return home excited about what God is doing in other churches throughout the region and with a renewed commitment to win their villages for Christ.

As I write these words, our missionaries and evangelists continue into remote communities throughout southern Africa. Many of them still travel by foot and are away from their homes for weeks at a time. They sleep in open fields, getting drenched when it rains and burned by the sun; they deal with snakes, wild animals and other hazards. Some travel by bicycles that have been provided through Iris Ministries. I wish we had the means to give a bicycle to every pastor, evangelist and missionary who does not have a car. A bicycle makes it so much easier to travel Africa's back roads.

Of course, many of Africa's villages remain desperately in need. They are hungry, so we send them food. They suffer and die due to a lack of basic medicine, so we send them the pharmaceuticals they need. We are showing them that God cares about their needs and wants them to be healthy and happy—and they are responding.

We are doing all of this with an urgency, because we are convinced that the end times are upon us. Jesus said, "And this gospel of the kingdom will be preached in the whole world as a testimony to all nations, and then the end will come" (Matthew 24:14). We are running out of time.

Let me close by sharing a vision God recently gave me. I saw fire sweeping up from South Africa across the continent and then on to Jerusalem. Then I saw fire igniting in several other countries, spreading from each and heading to Jerusalem: Canada, the United States, Great Britain, South Korea, Taiwan. Then I saw thousands of people, perhaps millions of people, walking with the fire, praising God for the return of Christ and the establishment of His Kingdom on earth. What I saw convinced me that Christ's return is imminent. His return will bring tremendous joy to those of us who know Him but terror to those who do not. The situation is urgent; time is short. We must do everything within our power to reach the lost and help them be ready for the Great Day that is about to come.

Surprise Sithole was called by the Lord Jesus Christ at the young age of fifteen, when the Lord told him to leave everything behind, follow Jesus and preach the Gospel wherever he went. Leaving his family and all his possessions, he took up his cross to follow the Lamb wherever He goes and has never looked back.

In 1997 God sovereignly connected Surprise with Heidi and Rolland Baker of Iris Ministries. Surprise now serves as the International Director of Pastors for Iris Ministries, in which he oversees the rapidly spreading revival in Africa that has witnessed over 15,000 new churches birthed since the year 2000. Together with his wife, Surprise also runs his own base in South Africa, where they live with their four children, Enoch, Love, Israel and Blessing. He travels the world as an international speaker, bringing revival and the refreshing rain of Holy Spirit wherever he goes and demonstrating the living power of Jesus with signs and wonders. Surprise loves Jesus more than life itself, and this all-consuming passion drives him to the darkest and most unreached areas of the world. He has but one driving passion and desire: to see Jesus' name lifted high and to see "the earth . . . filled with the knowledge of the glory of the LORD as the waters cover the sea" (Habakkuk 2:14).